MASTERS OF THE HARMONICA

MASTERS OF THE HARMONICA

30 Master Harmonica Players Share Their Craft

Margie Goldsmith

MOUNTAIN ARBOR
PRESS
Alpharetta, GA

These interviews have been edited and condensed by the author.

Copyright © 2019 by Margie Goldsmith

All rights reserved. No part of this book may be reproduced or transmitted in any form or by any means, electronic or mechanical, including photocopying, recording, or any information storage and retrieval system, without permission in writing from the author.

ISBN: 978-1-63183-646-6 - Paperback
eISBN: 978-1-63183-647-3 - ePub
eISBN: 978-1-63183-648-0 - mobi

Printed in the United States of America   091719

∞This paper meets the requirements of ANSI/NISO Z39.48-1992 (Permanence of Paper)

Cover and back cover design by Ojedokun Daniel Olusegun. Cover photograph by Kris Ciesliga, back cover photograph by Matt Peyton Photography.

*To my sister Lynne and her partner, Howard,
for their ongoing love and support.*

If you're gonna play a note, play the hell out of that goddamn note. You can take one note and upset a house. Play that damn note; don't let the note play you.

—Sonny Boy Williamson II (Rice Miller)

Contents

Preface xiii

Chapter 1
    Cheryl Arena: Baddest Harp Player 1

Chapter 2
    David Barrett: Minimizing the Bumps and Bruises 11

Chapter 3
    Sugar Blue: The Harmonica Wizard 19

Chapter 4
    Billy Branch: Ambassador of the Chicago Blues 29

Chapter 5
    James Conway: Deadly Druid of the Harmonica 39

Chapter 6
    Magic Dick: Lord of the Lickin' Stick 49

Chapter 7
    Carolyn Dolan: Master of Roots Music 59

Chapter 8
    Lee Edwards: The Yoda of the Harmonica 69

Chapter 9
    Rick Estrin: Legendary Showman 79

Chapter 10
    Joe Filisko: Master of the Traditional Harmonica 87

Chapter 11
    Jon Gindick: Pioneer of the Jam Camp　　　　　97

Chapter 12
    Dennis Gruenling: Jump Swing BadAss　　　　107

Chapter 13
    Adam Gussow: The Blues Professor　　　　　　117

Chapter 14
    Filip Jers: The Swedish Harmonica Sensation　　125

Chapter 15
    Buzz Krantz: The Santa Claus of the Blues　　　135

Chapter 16
    Howard Levy: Jazz Harmonica Virtuoso　　　　145

Chapter 17
    Delbert McClinton: At the Top of His Game　　155

Chapter 18
    Charlie McCoy: His First
    Harmonica Cost Fifty Cents and a Box Top　　165

Chapter 19
    Charlie Musselwhite: King of the Blues　　　　175

Chapter 20
    Paul Oscher: Keeping It Real　　　　　　　　　185

Chapter 21
    Rupert Oysler: Harmonica Zen Master　　　　　195

Chapter 22
    Todd Parrott: Inspirational Virtuoso   203

Chapter 23
    Annie Raines: Queen of the Blues   213

Chapter 24
    Jason Ricci: Standing
    Shoulder to Shoulder with the Greats   221

Chapter 25
    Wade Schuman: The Pied Piper of Hazmat Modine   231

Chapter 26
    Indiara Sfair: Harmonica Goddess   239

Chapter 27
    Ronnie Shellist: Global
    Blues Harp Summit Ambassador   247

Chapter 28
    Richard Sleigh: Intrepid Harp Tech   257

Chapter 29
    Kim Wilson: Soul of the Fabulous Thunderbirds   267

Chapter 30
    Winslow Yerxa: The Musician's Musician   277

Acknowledgments   287

Preface

I never really played an instrument. As a kid, I had a few piano lessons but hated to practice, so I stopped. As a teen, I learned three guitar chords, but that was as far as I went. In my twenties, I tried the five-string banjo, but I was so terrible that even the chipmunks ran away. In my thirties, I sent away for a book, *How to Play Blues Harmonica*, which included a free harp, and met the author, Jon Gindick, in San Diego, who gave me a free lesson. But when I arrived back home in New York City, I didn't have the patience to practice the little lick I'd learned.

Years and years later, traveling the world as a writer on assignment, I thought, *Wouldn't it be great to be able to play harmonica to children whose language I don't speak?* So I decided to take up harmonica at an age most people retire. I signed up for Jon Gindick's Blues Harmonica Jam Camp in Clarksdale, Mississippi. The cotton was in full bloom, the days balmy, and the Shack Up Inn, where the camp was held, irreverent and funky. There was a wonderful comradery, and everyone applauded us raw beginners who struggled to draw the two-hole.

When I returned home to NYC, I found out about Lee Edwards from Wales, who taught blues harmonica via Skype. What could a Welshman possibly know about the blues? Everything, it turned out. He helped me advance from a half-baked beginner into an intermediate player, making each step along the way fun and doable. I am still taking lessons from Lee, and while he continues to call me the most impatient person he's ever met (completely true), he inspires me, and under his guidance, I continue to make progress step by step.

Eight years ago, I became a member of SPAH (Society for the Preservation and Advancement of the Harmonica) and wrote for their magazine, *Harmonica Happenings*, where most of the interviews in this book originated. I am so grateful for all the great

Masters of the Harmonica

harmonica players and teachers I met there who have shared their time, knowledge, and inspiration to make this book possible. The only thing I regret is that I haven't been able to fit in *all* the great masters who belong in this book. I plan to do that in the future.

Chapter 1

Cheryl Arena: Baddest Harp Player

She's been called a blues harmonica queen, a musical standout, the baddest harp player—male or female—heard in many a year. Boston-based Hohner endorsee Cheryl Arena is a versatile songwriter, vocalist, and harp player who tours, records, and teaches. "She may be from Boston," says Johnny Rawls, "but her heart's from Mississippi." Arena has recorded on several CDs and has a solo record, *Blues Got Me*, with seven original songs and about which Charlie Musselwhite says, "Cheryl sounds better than ever on *Blues Got Me*; great harp tone and she doesn't overplay, which is refreshing."

The *New Hampshire Sunday News* calls Arena a "musical standout," and *Blues Revue* calls her harmonica playing "rich and tasty." *Blues Beat* says, "Watching Arena's energetic performance for one set is enough to exhaust you." Frank John Hadley of the former *Boston Phoenix* says, "No BS, just night after night delivering the goods in clubs, winning over audiences from Beantown to Florida."

Since 2001, Arena has taught harmonica lessons privately and to groups. In 2007, Jason Ricci introduced her to Jon Gindick, who was holding a harmonica jam camp in Dallas, Texas. Now, in addition to recording and performing, Arena is a mainstay at Jon Gindick's Blues Harmonica Jam Camps, teaching both harmonica and singing three times a year in Clarksdale, Mississippi, and Ventura, California. No matter where she's performing, Arena's harp is always in her pocket, ready for the next musical adventure, such as the new CD on which she is working, hopefully for release soon.

When were you first exposed to music?

I played accordion when I was nine years old in second and third grade, my first instrument. I also took tap-dance lessons, which, in hindsight, probably helped my internal rhythm. There was always music in our house, but no one played any instruments.

How did you happen to play accordion?

I wanted to play piano, but my parents were not real supportive. My grandmother had a music teacher friend and he had an extra accordion lying around, so I took accordion lessons thanks to my Polish maternal grandmother. My dad's side of the family was Sicilian, so I think they thought the accordion would be appropriate.

And why were your mother and father opposed to the piano?

They said I wouldn't stick with it. It's not like they didn't like music. They were into all types of music. They used to go to the Newport Jazz Festival every year, even when my mom was pregnant with me, so maybe music got into me before I was even born. I was exposed to a wide variety of music growing up. As a kid, two of my favorites were Billie Holiday and Louis Armstrong. I used to try to imitate Louis singing "Hello Dolly," holding a handkerchief to wipe my forehead while pretending to play the trumpet. Being rebellious and them not being supportive may have even pushed me harder to prove them wrong. "You won't stick with it," they said. "Well I'll show ya!"

What was your next instrument?

I played harmonica for a year when I was fifteen because it was the only instrument I could afford to buy on my own.

And you only played it for a year?

Yes, because being self-taught, I didn't know you needed different-key harps for different keys of songs. All I had was one harmonica in the key of G, so I would get very frustrated because I had a good ear and knew when it didn't sound right. The only time it sounded good was when I just happened to be in the right key. Then, on my sixteenth birthday, my boyfriend bought me a guitar, and I started playing guitar and put the harp down.

Were you just playing, or were you singing too?

No. I didn't start singing till much later. I played guitar for about twelve years, and then I started playing bass because everybody told me that I had good rhythm and that I'd be a really good bass player.

Are you self-taught?

Yes, on harmonica I play totally by ear and feel. I have a hard time reading tab. I used to run sound and lights for bands before I became a professional musician. I was playing guitar back then, but I was a "closet player," too shy to get on stage. I would jam with the musicians I worked for, and they would show me guitar riffs, plus I took some guitar lessons.

You gave up your G harmonica for guitar. So, when did you take it back up and why?

In 1987, I went to a blues jam with my bass, and there was a harmonica player with a case full of harps. I asked him, "Why do you need so many harps?" And when he explained, it was like a lightbulb went off in my head. I went out the next day and bought a few different keys and quickly found out that the harmonica was my instrument. It always was.

Did you eventually take harmonica lessons?

After I had been playing for ten years, I took five lessons from Sonny Jr. in Connecticut. It helped A LOT. He helped me break some bad habits I had developed. I still have the cassette tapes of our lessons. There was no internet then, so I had to drive almost three hours each way for lessons. Nowadays you can look anything up on the internet.

You started singing around 2000. What made you suddenly start?

I was in a band with my ex-husband, who was the guitar player. When we split up, I had to start my own band because as a harmonica player, if you are not fronting the band, it's very hard to find gigs. So, I started singing out of necessity so that I could continue to gig.

When did you start writing music and why?

I wanted to do original tunes. I didn't want to do a record with covers, but I may end up doing that because I am tired of waiting. I need to do a new CD.

Which do you like best: singing, writing, harp playing, or any of the other instruments you learned?

I love playing harp, but I love playing bass and drums and singing, too. I love it all, but harmonica is number one because I've put the most time into it. But I just love making music, period.

Your first jam was Blues Monday night jam at Wally's Café in the South End of Boston.
Were you jamming just on harp? What did you do?

I started a blues jam because after playing for about three years, I'd go to jams and get frustrated because I had to sit and wait, wait, wait, and finally, a friend who felt the same way said, "Hey, let's start our own jam." So, we did. I was in the house band and I kept it going for three years, then it was time to move on.

You next played at Marketplace Café in the historic Faneuil Hall, an invitational jam.
What was the difference between that and Wally's?

Big difference. After I left Wally's, this guy who used to come in all the time tracked me down and asked me if I would do a jam at the place he was bartending, the Marketplace Café in Faneuil Hall, Boston. I said I'd rather do an invitational jam, meaning I'd book a band of professional musicians, different people every week, so the music would have variety and a higher quality. I learned so much in those years, and it was pretty magical at times and very successful. It lasted almost six years until the place changed owners and stopped having music.

And then what did you do?

I was playing in a band touring up and down the East Coast. We also played all over Florida to get out of New England for the winter. Then we toured in Mississippi and Memphis, we played on Beale Street, at the Black Diamond Club and B.B. King's and Rum Boogie and Blues City Café. We played in Jackson, Mississippi, and at the King Biscuit Blues Festival in Helena, Arkansas. And while on tour, if we had a Sunday night off and found ourselves anywhere close to Junior Kimbrough's Juke Joint, we'd go and sit in at the blues jam. That's how I got to be friends with R. L. Burnside. I really dove into the blues, not just the music, but the history and the people that created it, because I love it so much.

When did Jason Ricci introduce you to Jon Gindick?

I was living in Dallas in 2007, and they were doing a workshop there. I went in to visit with my buddy Jason. The first thing Jason says is, "You should give Jon one of your CDs and maybe he'll hire you as a teacher and then come back tomorrow and sit in at the jam." A few weeks later, Jon called and asked if I wanted to do a camp in Florida. That was the first one, and I've been doing them ever since, every single one. And I LOVE it!

And in addition to teaching at Jon's camps, you teach privately?

Yes. By Skype and for locals, at my house. I also teach blues ensembles at Morningside Studios in Arlington, Massachusetts.

What kind of harps do you play?

Marine Bands, Hohner.

I am told they are right out of the box. Why are they not customized?

Because customized harps are a luxury I cannot afford at the moment. The harps that are redone play really nice, but they wear out just as fast. A long time ago, I used to have customized harps from Richard Sleigh, and they were great, but then he got super busy, so the wait time was too long. I can play the ones that are right out of the box just fine.

Why are there so few women harmonica players?

I have no idea. There are more than you think. I mean, I am on a CD, *Blues Harp Women*, that Ruf Records put out, a two-CD set with all female harmonica players. There are thirty-one female harmonica players on this two-record set, and I know there are more out there.

Do you practice scales?

Sometimes—mostly when I'm teaching them.

Do you practice?

Yes, of course, but my practice comes from teaching and also from playing. I play all the time. I make my living playing, so I play as much as possible. I practice by learning new tunes. I'm constantly working on expanding my repertoire so I can play new tunes at my gigs. I enjoy the challenge of learning new material, and I'm always striving to be a better musician; the learning never really ends, and that's the beauty of it.

And when you are playing sometimes, do you ever improvise, or you are sticking to the riffs on the songs?

I always improvise. That's what blues is: a feeling.

But do you find that you are improvising based on the riffs you've learned, or is it coming from somewhere inside you?

Well, I mean, I think that most of it is coming from what you've already learned. It just gets into your subconscious, and then it comes out. But I mean, you can take a lick and change it by changing one note, so you can have somebody else's riff, but you can play it with a different cadence or with less notes or more notes and it becomes something else. There are only so many notes in the scale, so there are only so many ways you can rearrange them. I initially try to learn stuff note for note, but then it always seems to evolve into my own take on it.

Have you ever had a period when you were uninspired? If so, what did you do to get over it?

Try to learn new stuff or write or go listen to people that inspire me. Anytime I feel down and out, playing or listening to music is the cure for me. It always makes me feel better.

You mentioned before that you'd never make it as a harmonica player unless you could sing. So, let's talk about the singing.

Well, I mean, it's not "never make it." You might not get as many opportunities to play. Look at all the harmonica players out there—most of them sing, but there are a few who managed to get lucky, like Willie Nelson's harmonica player, Mickey Raphael. He just plays harp, he doesn't sing, so he's got the cushiest job. I would love to be a side man and just play harp.

Why?

Because being a singer and being a leader of a band is a lot of weight on your shoulders. Being a sideman is easier. You can just show up and play music. When you're a leader, it's like herding cats. You have to get the gigs too. It's just a whole ball of wax about which people have no idea unless they do it. They think, "Oh, you're a musician, that's fun, you have a fun job." And granted, it *is* fun, but it's also a lot of work. To me, working on music is fun—the business end of music is pretty brutal.

Do you practice singing, or do you just sing?

I do warm-ups now since I started teaching singing. As I learn more about how to teach singing, I find a lot of it is similar to harp, because it's a lot to do with breathing and learning to control your air and breath from your belly. When I started teaching harmonica, it made me a better harmonica player because it made me stop and think about what I was doing. So when our singing teacher at jam camp couldn't make it, I asked Jon Gindick if I could give it a shot, and just as I did with harmonica, teaching singing has made me a better singer. Now I warm up before I sing. I never used to do that. I do warm-up vocal exercises when I'm driving in the car or in the shower before I go to my gigs, and I'm constantly looking for new ways to help my students improve on their singing, which in turn helps me with mine.

What has music done for you?

Music has given me a purpose; learning how to play an instrument and play it well has made me feel good about myself. It makes me happy. Whenever I'm down, I can always depend on music. It saved my life. Who knows where I would be or what I would be doing? Music is a healer; it's good for the body and soul. I'm happiest when I'm playing A LOT! Music has also afforded me so many great life experiences, like traveling throughout the States and parts of Europe, and meeting and playing with all kinds of people, including some pretty colorful characters. For me, it's a gift, a blessing that I never take for granted and always appreciate. It might sound like a cliché, but music truly is the gift that keeps on giving.

Chapter 2

David Barrett: Minimizing the Bumps and Bruises

Grammy-nominated recording artist David Barrett is the world's most published author of blues harmonica lesson material. He is also the first to write books teaching traditional blues harmonica technique and approach, beginning with his first book, *Building Harmonica Technique*, which was published at the age of twenty-one. Since then, he has published over seventy books/CDs/DVDs, mainly for harmonica, with a few for other instruments. Twenty-two years later, David Barrett's books remain the only ones that teach both intermediate and advanced material for harmonica. Joe Filisko calls Barrett the world's most accomplished teacher of blues harmonica, and Steve Baker says that Barrett's online blues harmonica school is the best in the world.

Gary Smith, who was Barrett's first harmonica teacher when Barrett was just sixteen years old, says, "He was very intelligent, a fast learner, and he could duplicate anything I played. Within a couple of years he had musical mastery and complete control of the instrument. The really amazing part is what he has created in his School of the Blues. It was unheard of for people to get blues lessons—he has so much energy it blows out of his harmonica into other assets of life. He picked up acoustic bass and mastered that within months; he also plays other instruments—I'm in awe of him."

Aki Kumar, a former student of Barrett's, says, "David is one of the very best teachers in the world—if you don't get good fast, then you're doing something wrong. He made me want to get better because he's such a phenomenal player himself. He fostered this hunger; in every lesson he revealed a new secret."

In 1994, Barrett started the Harmonica Masterclass Workshop, the first to focus on blues harmonica education. Eight years later, he founded School of the Blues in San Jose, California. His newest comprehensive online school for all levels of harmonica playing is BluesHarmonica.com. Barrett, who studies martial arts and holds black belts in two disciplines as well as BuSaBumNim instructor level, often uses martial arts analogies when teaching harmonica.

When and how did you pick up the harmonica?

I'd played saxophone first, and then trumpet in the school band, and quit, but I wanted to stay with music. At the age of fourteen, I picked up the harmonica and learned from a Mel Bay book. I heard blues harmonica soon after that, in the 1986 movie *Crossroads*, and knew I wanted to play that style of music, so I recorded all the harmonica parts and tried to figure out what they were doing. That started my journey listening and copying LPs and learning from these recordings. When I was sixteen, I took my first lesson with local harmonica legend Gary Smith and learned how to really control my bends and tongue-block.

You started teaching harmonica when you were eighteen?

There were no books teaching blues music or any of the techniques, such as tongue-blocking, a core technique in blues harmonica playing. None really described how to bend beyond basic vowel sounds, so I started writing exercises and licks. I taught two workshops a month, and in one each month I'd focus on one technique and present it with written material. At the end of the year, I put it together into book form and Mel Bay published it.

When did you start the Harmonica Masterclass Workshop?

In 1994. I wanted to give my students the opportunity to work and learn from other harmonica players so they weren't just clones of me. Lee Oskar was very instrumental in making that first workshop successful. Eighty-five people signed up for this little workshop, and I thought, *Wow, there's really a need for this.* Eventually, I was doing up to six different workshops across the US a year, plus my private students, plus managing a music store, which helped me learn a lot about the music industry and the music business.

Then, in 2001, I had a vision of taking the top-notch music instructors in the Bay Area and starting a school focused on blues. We could all work together in regard to jam sessions, student concerts, and give our students a community.

I opened the doors to School of the Blues in San Jose in 2002. Students take private lessons, join jam sessions, put on student concerts, and I do a quarterly harp night. We also have a performance-training class to teach students how to feel comfortable playing with a pickup band.

Why BluesHarmonica.com?

The book market was starting to slump because of the internet and YouTube, and websites doing effective online learning for other instruments were just starting. As a teacher, it gives me all modes of learning to work with: video, music to study and exercise, PDFs, MP3s, slow-downs, jam tracks, and interviews to interweave with the lessons. It took me about five years to get all the core lessons on the website. I knew what they were going to be, so I was able to interweave those well, even with the interviews. What was a little bit daunting was that I was going to have to rewrite everything that I'd ever done, but I promised myself I would enjoy the journey, and if I thought it would be cool, then put it in; it's allowed me to be really deep on the lessons.

How does the website work?

People choose a subject that's of interest out of all the studies. For instance, students learn a study song, and once they feel pretty confident with it, they record themselves to the provided jam track and submit it to me for my review. I listen and give suggestions. Sometimes it's about rhythm, or about technique. The reason why I have them go through the recording process is usually they'll do it once, listen back, and will recognize some areas that need work. And they circle them and then get to work. Which is exactly the way you learn. So without me even saying anything, usually by the time I get the recording, they've already gone through that self-discovery process of fixing the things that needed to be fixed, and by the time I get it, generally I can focus on what they're not capable of hearing. This process helps to foster self-sufficient studiers, though students can ask me questions any time, of course.

And you have other experts on the site?

I know a little bit about most things, but there are those who specialize in them. For example, if people have questions about microphones, there's Greg Heumann on the site, and I pay him—not a lot—but he also answers questions because he's an expert on that subject. Skip Simmons is an expert at repair and things about tube amps. Winslow Yerxa is the most knowledgeable guy I know about the widest array of harmonicas, models, and styles of music. He's there as a general expert to answer people's questions, because even though I can play and teach blues chromatic, there are some technique things that I have no business answering questions about. It's great for students to know they're going to get answers from respected experts. It's nice to have an A-team.

What is the difference between BluesHarmonica.com and the Levels of Achievement (LOA) program?

At BluesHarmonica.com, we can work on any subject at any time, and if you want to you can record yourself and submit it to me for my review. LOA lays out very specifically what to work on when, with the goal of motivating students. There's also a testing component—they're held to a standard.

Why did you develop this Levels of Achievement program?

I wanted to make what to practice as clear as possible and motivate people along the way, as well as help them become good harmonica players and well-rounded musicians. It gives students a social reward to post on Facebook, a pin they can wear at SPAH, for example, something like the martial arts belt system to inspire them to both set goals and achieve a small social reward. The lessons are divided into five main categories: technique development, solo harmonica study, accompaniment playing, improvising/songwriting, and music theory. Students work through levels one to ten and submit the assignments, forcing them to work on some subjects such as, for example, accompaniment playing. No one ever said, "Hey, you might want to listen to what Little Walter did behind Jimmy Rogers or Muddy Waters." Also, most people won't do music theory, but it's part of the program. And that's been the benefit. What I'm seeing now that it's been around for a while, I'm starting to see a level of musicianship and understanding of music by my students on par with the other instruments, which is pretty cool.

What happens if a student fails to complete a level?

A student can resubmit as many times as they want. Because this is for self-growth, and the test is just me saying, "Here's the standard, work toward it, and if some area needs some help, let me help you through it." Rhythm is a common thing; I'll go through a couple submissions with them, and if they're still having difficulty with their rhythm, I'll recommend them to a local music instructor, a piano player, or guitarist and help get them started on some rhythm training programs.

Does level ten mean you're a professional musician?

It means you have mastered the techniques of tongue-blocking, bending, position playing (first, second, and third), their music theory is up to a level that they can communicate with and accompany other musicians well, they can song-write and improvise well. The requirement for level ten is they write an original instrumental in second position, third position, first position, and a self-accompanied instrumental to be done in a live performance. Just like the final black belt test, usually multiple days long, my black belt tests are commonly three days long with a public performance on the third day. In martial arts, when you get your first-degree black belt, that means you've mastered the basics. At BluesHarmonica.com, it's a little bit more than that, but the main thing is that they have everything that they need to become the next high-level pro in their area.

It's very common for professional players not to know how to play in another position, or their music theory knowledge is usually very weak, even in some of the very best of players. So because of this whole academic system, we're really raising the bar of what a player can do.

You are adamant that Levels of Achievement is the future of harmonica education. Why do you feel this way?

It's about the evolution of the availability of information. It started with scarcity (when there wasn't instruction of any type for blues harmonica) to availability (teachers and books) to abundance (online instruction and tens of thousands of YouTube videos), where it gets confusing and overwhelming—and that's where we are right now. There's so much material that students don't know where to start or what to work on because there's too much available. LOA narrows the focus and says, "You're going to focus on these elements at this level, get to work." Elements such as accompaniment playing and music theory are what our next generation of harmonica players need to up. The program offers a path that students can follow to make them better harmonica players, and hopefully keep them motivated.

My next step is to rerecord all the lessons. I've got almost four thousand videos on the website, and three months ago I started rerecording the beginning lessons to make them that much better.

If someone wants to become good, there's not going to be anything that gets in their way, but 80 percent of people are not going to have that internal fire that will drive them past those roadblocks and challenges that come their way. The challenging thing for me is refining the process in a way that minimizes those bumps and bruises along the way.

What is music for you?

It's something that is endlessly interesting to me, whether it's in my profession, blues harmonica, or any style of music. I love the structure of it, I love figuring things out, I love the simplicity of it, where it's more of an ethereal thing that just kind of washes over and gives you a feeling as opposed to an analytical thing that we as musicians and writers commonly get into. I love helping people in their journey to something that they're very passionate about.

As a performer, I just love blues harmonica music, especially the traditional post-war Chicago blues with a West Coast twist. The blues harmonica is just a cool sound, and there's just something about it. From a personal perspective, I love the music. From a business perspective, I'm very fortunate to be able to make a living in the field about which I'm still passionate, and from a financial standpoint, it's nice to be able to make a living and support my family in the field that I enjoy.

Chapter 3

Sugar Blue:
The Harmonica Wizard

Photo courtesy of Joseph A. Rosen

Grammy Award–winning harmonica virtuoso Sugar Blue was born Jimmie Whiting and raised in Harlem, New York, where his mother was a singer and dancer at the Apollo Theater. He spent his childhood among the musicians and show people and decided that he wanted to be a performer. He would win the Grammy

Award in 1985 for his work on the Atlantic album *Blues Explosion*, recorded live at the Montreux Jazz Festival.

Blue, as he is known, also recorded on Willie Dixon's Grammy-winning *Hidden Charms* album in 1989. He often performed live with the Rolling Stones and can be heard on *Some Girls*, *Emotional Rescue* and *Tattoo You*. He has performed on festival stages with Muddy Waters, B.B. King, Art Blakey, and Lionel Hampton; sat in with Fats Domino, Ray Charles, and Jerry Lee Lewis for the Cinemax special *Fats Domino and Friends*; and has appeared on screen and in the musical score of Alan Parker's acclaimed 1987 thriller *Angel Heart*, starring Robert De Niro.

Blue has played and recorded with musicians ranging from Willie Dixon and Stan Getz to Frank Zappa, Johnny Shines, and Bob Dylan, but is perhaps best known for his signature riff and solo in the Rolling Stones' hit "Miss You" from their *Some Girls* album. He received two nominations at the Junior Wells Harp Awards. He is featured in the film *The Perfect Age of Rock 'n' Roll*, along with Pinetop Perkins, Willie "Big Eyes" Smith, and Hubert Sumlin.

It has been said that Sugar Blue "bends, shakes, spills flurries of notes with simultaneous precision and abandon, combines dazzling technique with smoldering expressiveness, gives off enough energy to light up several city square blocks, and sings too!"

Your mother was a singer and dancer at the Apollo, and you spent your childhood among musicians including Billie Holiday.

Yes, but I met Billie when I was maybe three months old. And the fact that I remember that has nothing to do with my memory. It's got to do with my mom telling me about it. When I grew up and I realized who Billie Holiday was, you could've knocked me over with a feather.

What made you decide you wanted to be a musician?

I fell in love with a song on my mother's record player called "PC Blues" by Billie Holiday's favorite classical saxophonist,

Lester Young. I asked my mother to play it over and over and over, and when she didn't, I learned to do it myself. And she said, "Boy, if you scratch my record, I'll kill you." That was in the days of the diamond stylus and high fidelity.

How did you end up with your first harmonica?

My sixth-grade teacher gave me a saxophone. I took it home and I'd play that thing from the time I got out of school till the time I went to bed. And that was my mother's breaking point. She disallowed saxophone in the house, so she took it from me. My aunt, seeing how miserable I was, bought me a harmonica.

Was it a Hohner? And are you a Hohner endorsee?

But of course. It's not a harp if it's not a Hohner.

Were you self-taught?

Yes.

And you played along with Dylan and Stevie Wonder when you heard the radio?

Yes. Dylan and Stevie Wonder and all of the cowboy movies. I loved cowboy movies because they all had harmonica in them.

And then you also became influenced by Dexter Gordon and Lester Young?

I'd been listening to Lester since I was about five or six because my mother was always playing the Billie Holiday–Lester Young duo things. I didn't get into Dexter until later in life, and actually even got to meet and play with him.

What was that like?

It's like when the littlest angel meets God. It was really fantastic because I had been listening to him since I was in high school, and

I am not a jazz harmonica player by any means. I played blues and R&B and rock 'n' roll, but Dexter played a helluva blues.

How would you describe your style?

It's the way I play. I listened to a lot of big bands and all the great blues harmonica players; I listened to everything I could get. When I finally got into blues, I listened to all of those guys and tried to style myself on Sonny Boy and Little Walter. One day I was playing with Larry Johnson, a great guitar player, and that night I thought I had come as close to playing like Little Walter as anybody could get, and he said, "You know, that was really good, you sounded like Little Walter." I was radiant. And he said, "But this is not what you want to play with me, this is Piedmont style and it doesn't go like that." And at that point I realized I had to find a way to play my way. I had to be myself.

You began your career as a street musician. Were you playing solo or with a street band?

I was playing with a washboard player, a guy named Washboard Doc, and playing with people that I met in the park, with anybody and everybody back in the early seventies.

And this was in Harlem?

No, but I met with a guy in Harlem, Sweet Papa Stovepipe, who was playing the blues—unheard of at the time, as it was the grand epoch of Motown. I'd heard very little blues, and never live. So I sat there with him the whole day, and he talked and we played. I never saw him again. Just a wandering minstrel. I started playing that stuff and hanging out in the West Village. The West Village is where I really started busking.

Where did you meet Dylan?

In the Village through a classic blues singer, Victoria Spivey.

We were all there listening to Willie Dixon, and she took me around to the back in the VIP section and introduced me to this guy and said, "I want you to meet my son." She said, "This is my son, Bob." And I am saying to myself, "That looks like Bob freaking Dylan." And she said, "He's the greatest harmonica player in New York City, and he's going to be on your next record." And I ended up in the recording studio, but the track that we did was not included on the record. It didn't come out until years later on *The Basement Tapes*.

You made your first recordings in 1975 with Brownie McGhee and Roosevelt Sykes. How did that happen?

Actually, my first recording was with Victoria Spivey. She introduced me to Roosevelt Sykes, and I was also playing with Louisiana Red. We went to Canada and recorded with Roosevelt Sykes and a bunch of really great players. That was Blue Labor Records. I will never forget that, because we used to call it Red Labor.

In 1976, you contributed to recordings by Victoria and Johnny Shines before moving to Paris on the advice of Memphis Slim. Why did he tell you to move to Paris?

I met him at the Top of the Gate, where he was doing a three-nighter. The second day, I got up the nerve to ask him to sit in, and he said, "Yes, come on. You can sit in, but if you mess up my set, you see this shoe?" And boy, did the man have some big shoes. He said, "If you mess it up, I am going to put it where the sun don't shine." He liked it. After, we sat down, I asked him, "Who do they like to hear play in Paris?" And he said, "They like Sonny Boy Williamson. Why don't you give it a shot?" About three weeks later, I was on a plane to Paris.

When you were in Paris, you hooked up with members of the Rolling Stones. How did that happen?

Actually, Keith had heard me play on a record that I'd done

with Louisiana Red in London. I was playing at a party where there were some close friends of Keith and Mick, and they said, "Well, hey, man, we're in the studio and you can play great harmonica, and they could probably use you." I thought the guy was pulling my leg. I gave him my phone number, and soon enough, I got a call from Mick Jagger, and next couple of days, I was in the studio with them. They were really going after a blues feel. It was an incredible, great opportunity.

You then appeared live with the Stones quite a few times, and they offered you the session spot indefinitely, but you turned it down. Why?

Because I wasn't going to be a Rolling Stone, and I had my own record, my own tunes, and my own ideas. All of a sudden, Keith was saying, "Would you like to record?" I took that opportunity to go record my first record under my own name.

You wanted to work with and learn from the blues harp masters, so you went to Chicago and sat in with Big Walter Horton, Carey Bell, James Cotton, and Junior Wells. What was that like and what did you learn from each of them?

My God. What didn't I learn, is more like it. These guys were all masters of the instrument in their own ways. I tried to internalize as much of their artistry as I could. I think James Cotton and Big Walter had the greatest influence over me. And I loved Junior, I just loved his stage presence, never seen anybody on the stage like that guy before.

What was it about him that was so appealing to you?

That he surprised them to the point of astonishment. He would take the harmonica out of his mouth and start making gestures that somehow enraptured the whole audience. You could hear a pin drop. And there was no music being played. And Junior was just there, making gestures with his hands and his body, and the audience was enraptured. It was like, "How does he do that?" It was like magic to me.

You spent two years touring with Willie Dixon, who was your friend and mentor, as part of the Chicago Blues All-Stars before putting your own band together in 1983. What did Willie Dixon teach you?

He taught me to be patient, he taught me to be quiet. He said, "Well, you're going to learn a lot more from listening than you will from talking, so be quiet." I loved it. He was something else. I mean, the man is a genius—songwriter, A&R, a life guide, and very much a father figure too. He taught me things that I didn't even realize he taught me. Years later, I'm going like, "Wow, Dixon said that!"

Can you give an example?

We were cutting a live record overseas. And he had been telling me, "Okay, you do this and you do that," and I was thinking to myself, *Hell, I'm the harmonica player. I know what to put where.* And so I ignored his teachings and went on with my own ideas as to how I should proceed, and after it was finished, we sat down and I was like, "Oh my God. I made a mess of this." At that point, I realized this guy knew what he was talking about and I had no freaking clue.

Of all the famous players with whom you've played, who's had the biggest influence on you? Is it Dixon?

Well, I guess it's got to be Dixon. He talked about writing songs—how to write songs and what to write about and why one should write about these things—and he gave me a lot of insight about how to create a musical muse.

You're playing Hohner harps. Are they custom?

They're straight from the factory.

Do you ever get nervous before going on stage?

Sometimes. I remember I was getting ready to go on stage with Fats Domino and Ray Charles and Jerry Lee Lewis. I was very nervous then. I was like, "Oh my God, Fats Domino and Ray Charles." Ray Charles is one of my favorites, for me, one of the greatest voices in recorded history of rhythm and blues, so to get the opportunity to play with them, I couldn't believe it. I was a nervous wreck.

Do you have any Ray Charles or Fats Domino stories?

No. My only story is that I was completely star-struck, and I remember just walking around in the green room and pinching myself.

Do you ever get up on the stage and think, "This is the same, I've been playing this before"? "I'm tired of it"?

No. Because I don't care how hard you work at it, you are never gonna play the same tune the same way twice. So you just play. A lot of times, the audience influences what you're doing and the other guys are behind you. No, I don't worry about that.

Do you practice?

Of course. You can't play if you don't practice.

Do you practice scales?

I practice scales. I practice songs. Sometimes I just take the instrument and just play around and do stuff, you know, just let the instrument do what it does, you know.

What do you want to be known for?

Well, I don't know. I guess the same things that people like about what I do. The songs that I write and the things that I play.

Just, basically, I'd like to be known for being a musician that knows and cares about the music. It's been said before by a much bigger musician than me, but I will repeat his words. As Duke Ellington said, "Music is my mistress." He wrote a book under that name.

What does music mean for you?

Music is my life.

Chapter 4

Billy Branch: Ambassador of the Chicago Blues

Photo courtesy of Joseph A. Rosen

While Billy Branch was still at the University of Illinois, he was discovered by Willie Dixon, "the father of modern Chicago Blues," who encouraged the young student to finish college. After graduating from college, Branch chose music over law school and toured with the Willie Dixon Chicago All-Stars for six years.

Masters of the Harmonica

Three-time Grammy nominee Billy Branch has recorded with Willie Dixon, Johnny Winter, Lou Rawls, Koko Taylor, Eddy Clearwater, Honeyboy Edwards, Syl Johnson, Lurrie Bell, Lonnie Brooks, Ronnie Baker Brooks, John Primer, and Taj Mahal. Considered the ambassador of the Chicago blues, he has played on over three hundred different recordings, including twelve under his own name. He served two consecutive terms on the Grammy Board of Governors and founded the Grammy Blues Committee, and has won multiple W. C. Handy Awards from the Blues Foundation, an Emmy, an Addy, two Chicago Music Awards, and numerous humanitarian achievement awards. His band, the Sons of Blues, has made over seventy international tours and delivered this cultural legacy around the world.

Branch is also a blues education pioneer who, since 1978, has taught the harmonica to almost a million children around the world. His internationally recognized Blues in Schools program teaches both young and old about blues as the roots of America's music. He has taught in the GRAMMY Museum's Music Revolution Project.

What was your earliest experience with playing music?

As a child, I taught myself harmonica. I had no ambition to be a professional musician.

How did you end up with a harmonica?

I just walked into a Woolworths and saw one. A little voice told me I could play it. I paid a dollar for it, put it in my mouth, and I could play it. I was about eleven years old.

So you're self-taught. How did you get so good?

Well, I'm blessed with a good ear. And I could replicate pretty much whatever I heard within certain limitations, but I could automatically play any melody. I construct solos melodically. I can duplicate what I hear.

You taught yourself how to bend and do overblows?

Blues was everywhere in Chicago. I listened to people like Junior Wells and Big Walter and Carey Bell and James Cotton, and over the years, found my way into the blues clubs. You would meet someone more advanced than you and you could say, "Man, that's sounds pretty cool, how do you do that?" I also met and learned from Charlie Musselwhite, Rick Estrin, and Jerry Portnoy as well.

So how did your career take off?

I was born in Chicago, raised in LA, and came back to Chicago to go to the University of Illinois. On August 30, 1969, I was at a festival, the greatest blues festival ever produced in history, by Willie Dixon. The blues was all around here and still is, but much more then. And after a few years, I ended up sitting in with people like Junior Wells, Lefty Dizz, and numerous others. I played with the great boogie-woogie piano player Jimmy Walker for years, and then after that I went with Willie Dixon. It was like a mecca here. I hung out at blues clubs at night and went to classes during the day. I hung out with Big Walter Horton, Robert Lockwood Jr., the Aces (Little Walter's band); I ended up recording with Koko Taylor, Son Seals, Lonnie Brooks, and Johnny Winter.

You joined Willie Dixon's Chicago Blues. How did that happen?

In college, there was a young lady on campus doing secretarial work for Willie Dixon, and I kept bugging her. "Wow! You work for Willie. Can you introduce me?" Finally she said, "Look, here's his number, you call him yourself." I called him and he said, "Hey! Come on down to my studio." His harp player at that time was Carey Bell, who happened to be out of town. They were practicing for a session and Willie said, "You got a harp with you?" So I practiced with the band and they said, "You know where Chess Studio is?" I said no. The next day, we did this recording session. Then maybe two years later, when Carey Bell quit, I was called to replace him.

What was the experience like?

I played with Willie roughly six years, and it was a fantastic learning experience. I thought I was pretty good, but found out very quickly that I didn't know as much as I thought I did. But Willie had a lot of faith in me, and he gave me encouragement and said, "You'll be all right." I persevered and got better. Willie was a great teacher, philosopher, and mentor as well as a showman, artist, and songwriter. It was one of the greatest experiences that you could ever have.

What was the most important thing you learned from him?

I learned the importance of the blues in American and world culture, the significance of its power and its impact on audiences around the world. Sadly, the blues is rarely seen on commercial television. Willie Dixon had a deep, profound love and respect for this African American cultural legacy, and he emulated that. I think that's what became my inspiration and my vision to teach children, because this music is so fantastic and so powerful, notwithstanding the fact that the blues is the roots of all of America's music: country, R&B, rock 'n' roll, jazz, hip-hop, everything, but sadly, it is so overlooked.

One of the things that strikes me the hardest is that some of the greatest musicians I knew died without recognition and without financial remuneration. They didn't get paid, and they're gone. You can possibly see clips on YouTube, but in most cases, if you missed seeing them live, you missed out. There were guys here in Chicago on whom I look back fondly and remorsefully; the guys back then we called mediocre would be the top of the heap now, because they were authentic blues guys and they all had their own styles.

In addition to Willie Dixon, there was Blind John Davis (almost like Ray Charles), Robert Lockwood Jr., Otis Spann, of course Muddy and the Wolf, Homesick James, Big Joe Wiliams—there were just hundreds, and they're gone. The most innovative of them all was the legendary Little Walter. He worked at Chess Records with Willie. I call him the Charlie Parker of the blues. He manipulated the distortion of the harmonica and mic like Jimi Hendrix did later with the guitar. They're all gone. I do my part in keeping the legacy, but these guys lived it. I didn't pick cotton and I didn't plow fields with mules, I didn't experience Jim Crow, I didn't have a fear of being lynched. Compared to them, I was born with a silver spoon. Dixon taught me to honor and respect those original blues men and women and to teach the next generations about them.

Do you practice anymore, or are you just busy playing so you don't need to?

Well, you can never say you don't need to practice, but I don't practice, per se, like I would like to. I have a goal to set up a practice regimen, but my practice is essentially on stage when I take risks on solos and I try different things. I try to do things that I don't normally do. Also, as I prepare to perform or record in other genres, I am stretched outside my normal playing style.

Does your improvisation come out of taking those risks?

This is where I think some people miss the depth of the tradition; the essence of the blues is like telling the story of African American history. In Africa, there was the griot, the storyteller, who conveyed the oral tradition, and that's how they preserved our history, which encouraged a cooperative community. You had to interact with each other. Then, to be able to do that, you sat around and you'd recite the history, and you'd recite it over and over and over.

There are some incredible technicians, like guys who have

mastered overblowing, who play way faster than I do, but the important element is that the essence of the blues is in the feeling; it's in the soulful expression. The soul of the music is when you evoke the most emotion. And while those aspects of technique certainly are essential to making you a rounded player, in the end, to me it is the expression of feeling that makes you a great blues player.

Do you teach blues harp by Skype? In person?

I've done both. I do it by Skype. If it's practical, I'm able to periodically teach lessons at my home. (For more info on lessons, email Billy at billybranchmusic@gmail.com.)

What's the best bit of advice you could give to someone just learning how to play blues harmonica?

While you may not have the benefit that I did being around all the great players, you do have YouTube. You can watch, listen, and study recordings and play along with them. Practice a particular solo or a particular song. I think Little Walter's "Juke" is a great challenge because it combines so many elements: you have melody, you have time, you have a classic example of breathing, and you have tone to emulate—you've got it all there. It's challenging, but it's a great thing to which to aspire. I've been playing "Juke" as long as I've been playing blues. I play it probably 95 percent note for note. I hear these little subtleties that I miss, but essentially, I play it as it was recorded. One of these days I'm going to get the whole thing down 100 percent, because Little Walter was the greatest exponent of the Chicago blues harp that ever lived.

How do you make intermediate players better? What's the best piece of advice you can give them?

Practice, practice, and every opportunity that you have to play with other blues musicians, by all means take it. The better the musicianship, the better your potential for advancing. To improve, you have to be able to play with good musicians. We're really blessed in Chicago because there are a multitude of great musicians playing authentic blues here.

What about advanced players?

If you're an advanced player, it's important to be gracious, approachable, and kind, because it's important to remember where you came from.

Have you ever had a period where you were just uninspired and you felt as though you were playing the same riffs?

Yes, I did, very much so. For quite a few years, I got kind of in a rut because I was doing the same weekly gigs. I think the release of our last CD broke that spell. I was forced to get the creative juices really flowing again and open up that fountain, so to speak. I was very proud of my album *Blues Shock*, because I wrote most of the material, both the lyrics and the music. And I am equally proud of my newest album, *Roots and Branches*.

What harp do you play?

Suzuki Manji. When Manji was still developing their harmonica, they pushed me to be a prospective endorsee, and they even used some of my input in part of their design. The engineer came to our house, and they sent prototypes based on my ideas and asked for my feedback each step of the way.

What do you think of the blues scene today?

In my opinion, it's in the transition phase. You're starting to see young people of all ethnicities in the blues scene, which we all know for the last twenty or thirty years has been dominated by people of non–African American descent. It is quite the paradox that black people don't listen to the greatest music on the planet, a music their ancestors created.

I'm optimistic about the direction the blues is taking. The blues is a vehicle for bringing diverse peoples together to either make music or enjoy it as an audience member. In the eighties and nineties, the blues fell out of favor with black folks, but we believed so strongly in our music that we took the blues into the black middle-class lounges on the South Side of Chicago. We were young and vibrant, and given the chance, we were going to put the blues in your face. When we arrived in the black clubs, they snubbed their noses at us, but after three or four weeks we had them every single time.

In general, African Americans were not listening to the blues; so what we were doing was worthy because everyone was into jazz, R&B, funk, or soul, and we were playing the down-home Chicago blues. We weren't dressing it up, we were just bringing it to them straight, and I'm very proud of that.

You should also be very proud of what you are doing with children through Blues in Schools. When did you start doing that?

In 1978, there was a residency available through the Arts Council, and I kept on through Urban Gateways. Lurrie Bell and I went to black schools all around Chicago and the suburbs. Little kids would shout, "Got my mojo!" Since then, I've done residencies all over the world.

What do you think is the future of blues?

The blues will never die. I think with the world's current situation, everybody has got the blues in some form. The blues is unique—it's the only music you can claim as an art form and as a feeling. You can't say, "I got the jazz," or "I got the hip-hop," but everyone gets the blues. That's why it's so universal, that's why everybody feels like they are entitled to play it. It's the most universal feeling, because it's a basic human emotion.

With the homogenization, commercialization, and bastardization of the commercial music we hear on the airwaves, people are hungry for something real and authentic, not manipulated by tuners and effects. Neither junk food nor junk music can sustain you—it tastes good initially, but ultimately you need some substance, so ultimately music lovers have to come to the blues.

What has music done for you?

Music has afforded me an opportunity to travel around the globe and given me the chance to have friendships with people around the world. Music has allowed me to affect and change the lives of many young people. Music has touched every part of my life. It's a great feeling when you see that you're able to bring joy to people's lives. I know the Creator has blessed me through the blues, and I am grateful for the joy it brings to the fans who come to hear me. The blues is primal and universal, and I am honored to be its ambassador, bringing it to people around the world

Chapter 5

James Conway: Deadly Druid of the Harmonica

Photo courtesy of Heather Miller

"When James Conway's name is brought up amongst accomplished players, sighs are let out, arms are tossed back, and heads go down. The dude is an enigma, a total maniac, and the techniques behind his music are *insane*," says Jason Ricci, who adds, "Conway is the king of tongue-switching. His octave leaps, effortless complex melodies, and chords are mind-melting to the harmonica player. He's the great, redheaded, ambidextrous deadly druid of the harmonica."

Brendan Power says, "Jim Conway has a fantastic ability with tongue-switching on the fiddle tunes, and I really like his use of the XB-40. He is not only a wonderful harmonica player, but also one of the nicest guys in the scene, always positive and friendly, musically open-minded, and encouraging of other players." Joe Filisko adds, "Jim Conway could have a page in *Ripley's Believe It or Not!* if folks were to find out what he has going with his tongue when he's playing. He is among the best Irish-style players that I have ever heard." And Howard Levy says, "It's really refreshing to hear someone playing Irish music with a bluesy attitude the way he does it on the diatonic."

Irish American Chicagoan James Conway plays diatonic and chromatic harmonica, flute, tin whistle, guitar, and bodhran. Conway is a virtuoso of fast-tempo reels and jigs, bending, trilling, and chording. He learned his techniques in the West Side blues joints of Chicago from such harp heroes as Junior Wells and Sugar Blue. His Chicago power trio, The Boils, is featured on five CDS (including *Mouth Box*, on which he plays Celtic harmonica), and he's working on a new CD. The Illinois Arts Council awarded him both a Fellowship Award and Master/Apprenticeship Award, and he is endorsed by Hohner Harmonicas.

What was your first exposure to music, and how old were you?

I was about six. I started off with the fiddle, but I couldn't get anywhere with it, so I took up the tin whistle and the bodhran, an Irish frame drum. My first teacher taught me traditional Irish dance tunes on the penny whistle, very similar to the harmonica— both are two-octave diatonic instruments and come in all twelve keys, but a D tin whistle is all you need in a traditional Irish session, the reason why I started off playing it.

Were your parents musical?

My mom is very good singer of Irish songs, and my dad plays

a little accordion and some treble harmonica. He always had a tremolo harmonica in the drawer; that's not why I started playing harmonica, though it might have had something to do with it.

Was it your idea or your parents' idea for you to play the tin whistle?

My parents wanted me to play Irish music. I learned it, entered many competitions, and did well. I played Irish music until I was fourteen, and then I got into folk and rock 'n' roll. I listened to Bob Dylan and Neil Young and bought an acoustic guitar and a harmonica holder. I was so impressed by Neil Young's harmonica playing and thought for sure he was using the most expensive harmonica available. I went to a music store and didn't know the difference between diatonic or chromatic, but they had chromatics in the $80–$100 range (probably now worth $200–$300). So I bought one, assuming that's what Neil Young used, and tried to figure out how to play it. With the poor, rough technique of a beginner, I quickly destroyed the valves on the chromatic.

When did the harmonica become important to you?

When I was nineteen, I heard Junior Wells play at Rosa's Blues Lounge and was blown away. I began a big blues journey and went to Rosa's every night and eventually got a job there as a doorman. Junior Wells, Carey Bell, and James Cotton would play there and give great tips to me and other beginners. I started practicing more, and eventually I heard Sugar Blue doing all this high-register stuff, the lightning-fast sixteenth notes, and tongue-blocking with the backup chords. Those high-register notes sounded a lot like my penny whistle, like the breakneck speeds of Irish reels, and also sounded a lot like the accordion in Irish music.

So how did you connect your penny whistle with the harmonica?

I started working on high-end riffs like Sugar was doing. I

discovered I could do all these jigs and reels on the harmonica that I'd been doing on the penny whistle. I thought I was going to take over the Irish harmonica world! This was before the internet. Little did I know that there was a handful of very good players already doing that, including Ireland's Murphy family and New Zealand's Brendan Power—but there weren't (and still aren't) too many of us.

Did you take your new sound into a band?

I formed an Irish band called Gan Ainm and started flaunting the Celtic harmonica but throwing a bluesy touch into it, which a lot of the purists didn't care for, and sometimes, still don't. If I go to these Irish sessions, get a little bluesy, and start bending, the old-time Irish guys say, "Damn it, Conway. You're throwing that hillbilly stuff into it now."

What kind of music do you like?

Of course I love Irish music, my heritage. I love acoustic folk music, and acoustic country blues of the finger pickers. I saw Honeyboy Edwards and wanted to learn how to make a guitar sound like two or three instruments with alternating bass and open tuning and sliding, so I researched that and bought recordings, everybody from Mississippi Fred McDowell to Blind Blake, Bo Cutter, Skip James, Blind Lemon Jefferson—pretty different from the Irish dance tunes.

How do you define yourself?

An acoustic musician who enjoys dabbling in Celtic, folk, old-timey, and country blues. I'm a happy musical camper when I have a balance between those styles, but mostly country blues. I do a lot of those covers from those older country blues guys.

So you play harmonica and guitar?

I sing and play guitar and have the harmonica holder . . . it's kind of a potpourri of styles, but mostly country blues. I throw in some Celtic pieces, some French Canadian harmonica numbers, and some folk numbers, but it's predominantly a mixture of country blues, Delta blues, and bluegrass. I whip out the penny whistle for a couple of numbers.

Are you still playing the bodhran?

I did a couple of YouTubes of me playing the bodhran while playing harmonica, and it's a really cool thing. I have to start doing more bodhran, especially with the harmonica holder and doing some jigs and reels and some solo harmonic pieces like the whooping harmonica, the foxtrots, and the train imitations with the bodhran.

How do you get your tempo?

These jigs and reels were designed for dancers, so I established a strong back beat with the harmonica using the rhythmic tongue-chording. I'm a tongue blocker, and I do everything tongue-blocked, from bends to overblows, overdraws—not that I use those things that much. But everything can be done with tongue-blocking. I show that to people when I'm teaching. The original design of the instrument—you see the little instruction manual on the older harmonicas that shows you how to support a melody with the tongue. I try to establish a tempo from playing by myself or playing with a drummer and guitarist to use those rhythmic chords and establish a good tempo, before blasting into the melody.

How do you get your extraordinary tone?

I think you can get great tone whether you're a lip purser or a tongue blocker. There are some purists of the Little Walter regime who say you must tongue-block to get good tone. I think you can get good tone with either pucker or TB embouchure. I get a better tone playing out of the side of my mouth with the tongue. Tongue-blocking is a great technique for rhythmically hitting chords and to support your melody, whether it's first position, second, or third, and that really drives the tune. A subcategory of tongue-blocking is tongue-switching, which enables a player to get from one end of the harmonica to jump over a bunch of holes very quickly just by a small maneuver of the tongue. If you didn't, you'd pick up unwanted middle notes and probably lose some timing by struggling to jump over those intervals.

Aren't you unique in tongue-switching? Aren't there very few people who can do it?

I learned it from Sugar Blue at Rosa's. When I heard him doing those fast jumps between low and high notes without moving his head or the harp, it just blew my mind. He taught me a lot of those things—that, and circular breathing and other cool harmonica techniques. I guess I am somewhat unique in using tongue-switching on the Irish tunes. Brendan Power and I do shows and seminars and really complement each other nicely. He does his Irish tunes so beautifully, but he uses pucker and I use the tongue block. So, when we play, the listeners can totally tell who's who, and it's like two different instruments.

The stuff I learned from Sugar Blue about tongue-switching makes me pick some of these Irish tunes that other players wouldn't pick that use pucker embouchure. They pick their tunes that have more "stepwise motion melodies" with no big intervals that would require tongue-switching. And if you can't do this tongue-switching, then it can sound pretty sloppy if you're trying to do a song with big interval jumps. So, I guess in learning to play these Irish tunes at speed, it's been a workout for my tongue, so I have a very powerful quick tongue.

Do you listen to anybody for inspiration now?

I still go back to Junior Wells and Sugar Blues; I like Big Walter a lot. I love Little Walter, but I still like to listen to Big Walter. Joe Filisko is an inspiring master, and I like obscure, solo harmonica players from DeFord Bailey to Gwen Foster. These are the guys I've done my best to steal. Winslow Yerxa turned me on to the old French Canadian recordings, music from Quebec. All these old tremolo players were doing really amazing, acrobatic tongue stuff with their leaky tremolos. There were many female players back then too, though mostly male players recorded. Mary Bolduc was a great player. I listen to those old recordings, and it's amazing—the performers go on three, four minutes with machine-gun-like tongue techniques.

Do you practice?

As much I can. We have three kids and I do have a day job, sadly. My wife and I are hopeful for me to get back into music full time again, but I always practice—especially at my job. I always carry two keys of harmonica and my phone is packed full of stuff. We live in a great time with gadgets and the internet and devices. The phone is just a great practice tool with slow-down programs and apps and YouTube. I'm working on some pieces and use thesession.org, which is a great site for jigs and realms and Irish tunes—really accurate versions of tunes, sheet music, and ABC tablature. I have little micro practices, even if it's a low-D harmonica on the subway that I take every day, just playing into my hands. The volume of low harmonicas is much lower than some of the cell phone chatter that is going on in the trains, so I never offend anybody with that.

When you're playing traditional Irish music, do you memorize all that, or do you improvise it?

You have to memorize it. These tunes usually have two, sometimes three or four parts, and each of the parts is repeated throughout—eight bars that are repeated. So there will be an A part, a B part, and AA BB are played pretty quickly. You play each of them three times. There's a lot of repetition, so these tunes aren't as hard to memorize as some would think. The melody is strictly adhered to, but everyone will ornament differently, so that's kind of how an Irish musician improvises . . . very different from the jazzer or blueser, who is composing solos instantly over chord changes.

How do you improvise?

I am constantly trying to increase my knowledge of my instrument with different chord progressions, scales, rhythms, etc. to become a better improvisor. When it's time for me to take a solo, I like to know the chords in the song and then quickly think about where those chords are on my harmonica. As I get older and wiser, I'm worrying less about dazzling the audience with speedy solos and trying to concentrate more on tasty, little, meaningful phrases. Occasionally, I like to punctuate the starts and/or ends of these phrases with techniques such as octaving or tongue trills to catch the listener's ear. Corky Siegel taught me a great lesson about improvising; he said, "The more you focus on dynamics, the better you'll improvise." He's right.

You teach harmonica?

Yes, I have students who come to the house regularly, and I'm a sub teacher at the Old Town School of Folk Music for harmonica, whistle, and sometimes guitar. I teach Skype lessons, and anyone who is interested can email me at harp3333@hotmail.com. I go over tongue techniques and how to use them on fiddle tunes and teach a plethora of other harp-related stuff.

What brand of harp do you use?

I'm endorsed by Hohner. I really like Special 20s and Crossovers, too. I play with a lot of other single-note instruments like fiddles and flutes, so I prefer an equal-tempered harmonica. It doesn't take me long to retune a Special 20 or Crossover to equal temperament. I'm fairly handy with basic harp maintenance. Richard Sleigh has taught me a lot over the years, and I have a lot of his tools.

I play a little chromatic harmonica. For some Irish pieces, I choose to play with the chromatic instead of trying to get those accidental notes with overblows. I like the Super 64, I like the CX-12s. I still have a handful of the, sadly, discontinued XB 40s, which are really cool harps. It's a great loud instrument to play at Irish sessions, where amplification is discouraged. Rick Epping invented them, and I think it's a great axe, which sadly didn't catch on.

What has music done for you?

Music has been the conduit to the two things that I love most: meeting people and travel. I guess I have the travelling Irish minstrel in my blood. Music has enabled me to meet people around the globe, and I gain respect from those people and have fun, magical moments with them.

Chapter 6

Magic Dick: Lord of the Lickin' Stick

Photo courtesy of Joseph A. Rosen

Richard Salwitz, known as Magic Dick, has been called "the best white musician to ever play blues harmonica." A founding member of the J. Geils Blues Band, it was his innovative harp playing that created the band's distinguishing sound of high-energy rhythm and blues and rock 'n' roll. In 1992, Magic Dick and J. Geils formed the band Bluestime, featuring Magic Dick on harmonica and vocals and J. Geils on guitar.

In 2016, Magic Dick partnered with award-winning guitar virtuoso and vocalist Shun Ng for their debut release, *About Time*, a collection of innovative interpretations of old classics and soulful originals.

What was your first exposure to playing a music instrument?

When I was three years old, my mother gave me a Hohner Marine Band harmonica, same as I use today. At nine, I started playing the trumpet and took lessons for several years. Then, in 1971, I studied with the head of the brass department at Berklee College of Music and decided to start over from the beginning and do it right. I still love the trumpet, and still fool around with it. I've learned about breath control from playing the trumpet, and I'm deeply into all the great trumpet players, starting with Louis Armstrong, Roy Eldridge, Dizzy Gillespie, Fats Navarro, and Miles Davis.

I also have a deep connection to the great jazz saxophone players like Coleman Hawkins, Lester Young, Sonny Rollins, and John Coltrane. Charlie Parker is at the top of the list as far as alto saxophone players, and his musical importance to me can't be understated.

I'm a true fan of the original bebop music that was formulated around 1945, the year I was born. When I was about nine, there was a ten-inch LP, *The Birth of Bebop and Blues*, that had some Dizzy Gillespie and Charlie Parker on it, and I wore out this record before I ever conceived of playing harp.

In your sophomore year, you switched to harmonica. Why?

I had been exposed to some early blues and folk blues recordings and was particularly attracted to the harp. Number one, it was really small, and you could keep it in your pocket. But more important was the way it sounded. Once I had that instrument in my hands, I just knew this was going to be big trouble in my life.

You were self-taught?

Back then, there weren't really any teachers. I was exposed to the prominent Chicago players such as Junior Wells and James Cotton on record, but I was really self-taught.

You switched to harmonica in 1968. You, J. Geils, and Danny Klein became founding members of the J. Geils Band. How did that happen? And how did you get so proficient on the harmonica so quickly?

I was going to college intending to become a physicist or engineer; I didn't really know which I wanted to be. I met J. Geils and Danny Klein in my freshman year. J. was playing acoustic guitar and Danny was playing a homemade washtub bass. We hit it off right away, and I think we all knew our college days were numbered. We quit school and moved to Boston and met the other band members. I never viewed myself as being a proficient-enough trumpet player, so I decided to be a harmonica player.

Touring with a full band led to jams with blues greats like Muddy Waters, John Lee Hooker, Junior Wells, and James Cotton. How did you happen to jam with them, and what did you learn from each?

In the late sixties, all the performing Chicago artists decided to leave Chicago and tour the country. They'd come to Boston and we'd be sure to see them. I finally got to meet Junior Wells and James Cotton. When I first met Junior Wells, I asked him about microphones and he said, "You gotta get yourself one of them bowl-shaped microphones." He was referring to the Astatic JT-30 mic, a crystal mic, as compared to the Green Bullet, a dynamic and much more rugged microphone. They have similar sounds and size, but they're different.

Did you get yourself a bowl-shaped mic?

You bet. I experimented with many, many different microphones and still do.

Do you tongue-block, or do you lip-purse?

I do both and can switch midstream. I think in the beginning, the player should decide upon one approach and stay with it for quite a while. But once you get comfortable with that, I recommend adopting the other approach so that you learn both, because there are certain articulations that require the use of the tip of the tongue, such as when you speak. You cannot form your words effectively without using the tip of your tongue. So if you're tongue-blocking, it's very difficult to use the tip of your tongue for articulations. Depending upon the type of articulator you are, I think that lip-pursing allows a much higher degree of that.

However, sometimes the advantage of the tongue-block approach is somewhat smoother, what's called the legato connection between notes, like slurring notes together where there's no silence between one note to the next.

Technique and articulation go together. And tone. Your tone is very much determined in part by whether it's lip-pursing or tongue-blocking because the dimensions of the inside of your mouth change with these different approaches. The instrument by itself, free of hands, is just one sound. Once you bring your hands around it and hold it in various ways, the sounds are quite different.

What do you love about harp?

I love the pure tone of wind instruments, which serve as a model for what I'm doing with the harp. As a player of a wind instrument, you need to be able to produce a beautiful tone. You can change things with the shape of your mouth, your hands, whether to use more air or less air. All of these things work in tandem with each other.

In 1971, on the J. Geils Band's second album, *The Morning After*, you included "Whammer Jammer." How did that come about?

That came about as a desire to create something new. We were playing in larger venues like stadiums, and sometimes there was a break in the set such as inadvertently or intentionally breaking the mic stand. So we needed to take a minute or two to fix something that broke, and that would interrupt the flow. This was the perfect opportunity for "Whammer Jammer." We needed it for the show.

And did you start improvising when the mic stand broke, or was it something you would plan?

In the beginning, Peter would call on me to just play something while they fixed the mic stand. The things I played were the things that became the inception of the ideas for "Whammer Jammer." The band and I worked on it in the same way that you create a song. It's not just an improvisation, it's composed. The arrangement moves it along in such a way that there's an inevitability to it. As a harp player, even though I've played it so many times, I still sometimes make mistakes on it—it's not an easy piece.

In 2016, you hooked up with vocalist-guitarist Shun Ng from Singapore. What's it like playing as a duo compared to an entire band?

It's much scarier because there's nowhere to hide. In a band, I can actually stop playing and things would go on. In a duo, everything is essential, which translates to a much higher degree of nervousness for me. But I'm getting used to it.

Do you ever get stage fright?

I wouldn't categorize it as stage fright, but I can get really nervous and be nervous all day long. If I have a gig coming up, my week prior to that gig is going to be very much determined by the fact that I've got a gig and I want to be really on top of my playing. So that means even more time practicing.

But very long practice sessions can lead to muscular tightness in the neck and upper back, so you need to be reasonable about your training. Don't practice when you're tired, or you'll make the same mistakes over and over again. It's very important to practice with full concentration. It takes a certain degree of warming up and doing it intelligently so you can work on it every day. Flexibility is important too. Keep your facial muscles toned. You have to learn to play cleanly and slowly before you can play fast.

How do you feel about touring?

Packing and traveling to me is the worst part of touring. Being on stage and performing is a tremendous amount of work, but I always try to go out there with the intention of having fun. That really makes a difference.

What year did the J. Geils Band break up, and why?

We broke up in '84, which I will characterize as irreconcilable differences, issues.

What was it like playing with the J. Geils Band?

There were considerable tensions in the band like any band, but when we hit the stage there was an outlet for it. We held back nothing; we gave it all. It was driven by our mutual love of the music and our shared musical roots. I don't know that I want to do a band again. I love this format of working as a duo. It's more challenging and more demanding. It puts my role on an equal plane. It's a different situation.

What's your primary interest?

My primary interest is in developing my playing of the chromatic and the diatonic further than I've gone. And that's exactly what I'm doing. I'm playing the chromatic harp way more than I ever have before. It's become my center focus.

We all want to get to this level of quality as soon as possible, so how does a harmonica player do that?

By focusing the attention on creating. The most important thing is to make the harmonica an object of obsession. I'm not just obsessed with the harp, I'm obsessed with music. The harp is just one of the ways that I make music.

What is your best advice for beginners? What's the most important thing you'd tell them?

The most important thing is to lay the groundwork for the instrument to become an obsession. You have to *teach yourself*. People will suggest, "Well try this, do this, do that." You can get together with a teacher, but you're the one who has to do it.

The way you do it is by trial and error. When you're practicing, experiment and listen carefully to the result. It's very easy to just noodle around with the instrument, holding it in your hands, making sounds, having fun with it, and you should continue to have fun with it; but you have to develop enough of an obsession with it that will automatically take you to anything you need to learn. I participated as a master instructor in harmonica classes, but that's not how I grew with my instrument. It doesn't mean that you as the student are going to digest it any more quickly than you can on your own. And now, there's so much information on the internet. There was none of that when I started.

Also, you need to play scales. People that get really good at playing their instruments have spent a good deal of time playing scales. You shouldn't view playing scales as drudgery, especially when you realize that all these musical phrases, things that you hear that you might love, are scale fragments. When you play scales, you need to learn to play these things as music. Not just "Oh, I'm doing this drill." It's very important. It's a totally different mindset to practicing.

You need to be able to start on any note of the scale and go up or down to the next note, and not make a mistake. That's what a professional player can do. I play exercises. I play a major scale in all its modes and move on and play all the keys in that way. That's really knowing the instrument. And when you can play that way, you can play anything. I'm not saying I'm there yet, but I know the route to getting there.

What's the most important thing you tell intermediates?

Don't listen to praise or criticism. If somebody tells you that you're great, don't believe it. If somebody tells you that you suck, don't believe it. You became an intermediate player because you were doing certain things right. In order to develop, you have to get beyond the intermediate stage, which takes a lot of practice and focus. That's why I say don't listen to people. If somebody says something nice about your playing, appreciate it for a second. But keep your objective focus on the instrument and the sound that *you* can produce on it. That's where your attention needs to be focused, not on getting good. It's good that you're getting good, but getting good is nowhere near good enough if you want to be great.

What about advanced players? What do you tell them?

Same thing. In fact, I would say the best thing that can happen to advanced players is to not think they're so advanced. As a musician, you never get to the end of the road.

Do you practice?

Yes, intensively and with purpose.

Do you practice songs or learn new songs? Or just practice riffs and runs?

All of it. When I first started out, I would just play riffs and things I learned from records and copy other artists, but mainly Little Walter and both Sonny Boy Williamsons. But my influences go beyond the harmonica players. The jazz horn players were the guys who influenced the harmonica players who influenced me.

I started by learning a particular piece or a chorus so I could sing what the part was, then learn to play it on the harp, and then learn to play it live. I had to be able to deliver it live without mistakes. I recommend to players who think they're advanced to examine how advanced they are, because you're not really very advanced if you can't play all the keys in every mode.

What harps do you play?

Mostly Hohner. I also have a full set of Lee Oskar harps that Lee gave to me, and I use some of those. I think that they're really good harps. Hohners are really good harps. I mainly like the Marine Bands, which include the Marine Band, the Marine Band Deluxe, and the Crossover. One day I might play this particular one, another day I'll play that particular one.

What does music mean to you?

Everything. It means a great deal to me emotionally and spiritually and physically. It's what fills my time. I don't have to look for something to do. I'm obsessed with every aspect of it.

Chapter 7

Carolyn Dolan: Master of Roots Music

Photo courtesy of Louis Holscher

Lake Tahoe–based performer Carolyn Dolan has been entertaining audiences for over thirty years as both a vocalist and harmonica player. Performing American roots music (jazz, blues, and country), she has opened for Bruce Springsteen's sax player, Clarence Clemons; sung alongside country singer Collin Ray; backed up the Gatlin Brothers; and played for the Western Swing Society with many of Bob Wills' musicians.

After leading folk and rock 'n' roll bands for many years, Dolan created the Outpsyders (*sic*), her original western swing, rockabilly, and bluegrass band. The band released two CDs and was voted Best of Tahoe Country Band in 1995 and 1996. In 1995, Dolan was voted Best of Tahoe Female Singer. For her outstanding contributions to preserving and promoting western swing music, in 2015 she was inducted into the Western Swing Hall of Fame in her hometown of Sacramento, California.

After twelve years leading and managing the group, Dolan decided to dive deeper into blues and created Carolyn Dolan and Big Red, in which she sung funky blues and soulful R&B while developing her unique harmonica style. In 2015, Dolan released her debut crossover jazz-blues album, *How Deep Is the Ocean*, with members of the Reno Jazz Orchestra and pianist Peter Supersano. The album is a mix of swing, jump blues, and sultry ballads, with a taste of R&B.

In addition to performing, Dolan is an early-childhood music educator, and for over fifteen years has taught toddler, preschool, and early elementary music programs throughout the South Lake Tahoe school district.

How old were you when you were exposed to music?

I grew up in Sacramento with every kind of genre of music in the house. My dad played his big band albums, Benny Goodman, and Count Basie music on the weekends, and my parents danced to it in the kitchen. My parents' music influenced me as a kid, as well as my older brothers' and sisters' music like the Beatles and the Dave Clark Five, the Rolling Stones—that was the popular music when I was growing up. We had music playing in the house all the time.

And when you were a kid, were you singing?

I was drawn to music from a young age. I was a dancer from age seven through college. My brother had a clarinet, and I tried out for fifth-grade band and loved it so much that I told my mom I wanted to take band in summer school. She about died, because I would never want to go to summer school, except I wanted to play with a band. The next year my parents got a piano and I started taking piano lessons. That's when everything opened up musically, because I began to read music, understand theory, basslines, chords, and harmony—it really opened the door to singing, writing my own stuff, and eventually, even though I was dancing, musical theatre in high school. So I was singing and dancing by my early teens.

Classical ballet or modern?

Everything: jazz dance, classic ballet, and modern. I was also heading down to the clubs to see what kind of music was happening, and that's where the whole harmonica story began. At eighteen, I went downtown to see this band called Little Charlie and the Nightcats play, and that's when everything changed.

Were you introduced to Rick Estrin?

I didn't know him at the time. I used to just go down and see the band; I was so wowed by the music. That was the first time I'd heard Chicago blues. I wasn't familiar with that style of music, but I was always into music, and that took it to the next level. I got so hooked on the band that even though I wasn't twenty-one, I'd go down with a fake ID and listen every chance I could. Rick and Charlie were already pretty established; the band was probably ten years into their career. And because of that band and music, I decided to pick up the harmonica and start playing.

How did this happen?

I had a good friend, Eric Wohlerberg, who played harmonica. I'd go to his house, and he played Sonny Terry and Brownie

McGhee records, which for me was more mind-opening music. Sonny Terry became another big influence of why I picked up the harmonica. I loved the country blues, and this influenced my playing it in folk bands.

Were you playing harmonica in folk bands?

I started singing in folk bands in Sacramento, and it was very fitting to add harmonica into a lot of that music.

How did you learn the harp?

I was self-taught, with the exception of a few lessons. My friend who had a harmonica showed me a few licks, and we practiced. Once I got into my own harmonica (Hohner Special 20), I could understand it being similar to playing the piano. I learned to play cross harp, second position, the blues style; you play a fourth above the key that the band is playing in. So, I'd be in my car playing a cassette tape of John Lee Hooker, trying to play along and figure out the licks and how to play the instrument with a band. I really learned by listening, and because I had an ear from playing piano and singing, it was easy for me to pick out the notes.

Besides piano and harp, do you play any another instrument?

I picked up the guitar in my teens and also played rhythm guitar in the country band the Outpsyders. Music was always natural for me to adapt an instrument to.

Do you consider your voice to be your first instrument and harp the second instrument, or vice versa?

I'd say I'm a singer that can dive into all kinds of genres, but I've always had the harmonica by my side to accompany me on stage.

Your first band played folk rock 'n' roll. So were you the front man?

We were like the Peter, Paul, and Mary folk group. I was more of a harmony singer, and I really enjoyed that.

When did you create the Outpsyders, and would you please explain the name?

While I was playing in folk groups, I was also playing in a rock band, and a few country players approached me in the late eighties. We decided to put together a country band: a six-piece western swing group with fiddle, steel, banjo, upright bass, and drums. I played acoustic guitar, harmonica, and sang. As we were putting the band together and forming our personality, we used to play so much "outside" the conventional way of playing traditional western swing, rockabilly, and bluegrass tunes that we called it the Outpsyders. It grew into a sort of "psychedelic/western" approach to the music. Our motto became "the Continuing Adventures of Texadelic Psycho Western." We didn't want to infringe on the original Outsiders name, so we changed the spelling and branded it for our group.

Twelve years later, you created Carolyn Dolan and Big Red. How did that affect your particular harmonica-playing style?

While I was leading the Outpsyders, some of us in the band also played blues gigs on the side. I picked up a bullet mic and started playing through an amp. I got into more of the dirty blues and bends and warbles. That took years. I had to work at the blues. It was a whole different approach than the two-hand grip of sweet country single notes and chunking out bluegrass rhythm chords.

Did you play with Rick Estrin?

No, we talked about getting together. We talked about my

taking lessons, but it never happened because he's on the road so much. I live in Tahoe. If he was in Sacramento on a regular basis, I might be able to catch him.

You are soon to be the first-ever female headliner for the Sun City Roseville Harmonicoots. Why are there so few women harp players?

That's the question that everybody asks me, and I don't know why. It has been a male-dominated industry for so long. Big Mama Thornton played harmonica, and there are women blues singers who played guitar, but not too many female harmonica players. That is changing. There are a few anomalies who just haven't been recognized as part of the bigger picture. When you're out front leading the band as a singer and harmonica player, it raises the bar. People love to see women playing harmonica!

Well, there's you, Annie Raines, Cheryl Arena, and Indiara Sfair. Do you know her music?

I really like Indiara Sfair. Hohner sponsors her. I think she's one of the more recognizable harmonica players that I've seen out there. Her technique is good, and she's putting out some really nice videos.

What kind of harps do you play?

I was recently endorsed by Easttop Harmonica Company. Also, I play through Greg Heumann's BlowsMeAway harmonica mic with the Heumann element.

Who do you listen to for inspiration?

Oh, geez. There's so many. Charlie Musselwhite, Mark Ford, Robin Ford's brother—a great harmonica player. Mark Hummel is another great player. They're all on the West Coast. James Cotton. Dennis Gruenling; I dig his jump swing approach on chromatic. And then there's George "Harmonica" Smith and William Clark. As soon as I heard his stuff, I was just knocked out. When I got into playing swing so heavily, I really wanted to understand it and to play more like those guys.

Do you practice scales?

On the piano, and I think about scales on the harmonica. For reference, when I'm performing, I'm in the moment and feeling the music with emotion. I'm thinking more about phrasing and saying something, much like a singer.

What's your daily harmonica practice regime, or is there one?

I do a little bit of warm-up before the show. When I have time and I'm not being a mom, I can sit down and think about some licks that I would like to learn, so I'll work on that and innovate, too. I listen to a lot of different harmonica players while I am driving to the gig, because that's when I have time to really listen to stuff. I get it in my head, and then practice is coupled with stage time.

I had the opportunity to play with Ronnie Shellist last year at the Hohner Road Show in Carson City. I started checking him out (www.harmonica123.com) and Adam Gussow and their online instructional videos. These guys are taking harmonica instruction to another level. We didn't have YouTube and instructors from all over the world to grab tips from back then. I was on my own listening to other players. But now, with these guys online, I'm starting to rethink a lot of my playing and become more of a technician.

Have you ever had a period when you were uninspired and you felt as though you were playing the same riffs every time?

Yes, definitely. I think having other musicians/harmonica

players to bounce off of is really important. That's how you get past those blocks.

What's it like being an opening act?

Humbling. You know that you are there for the headliner—you are the warm-up. So I appreciate those opening-act gigs, but then I also take it with a grain of salt because I know I am there for the support.

When and how did you become an early-childhood music educator?

I dreamed about playing the harmonica, and I picked it up. I had a dream about teaching kindergartners, and ten years later, I was teaching them. I wanted to teach music, so I went back to school and got into the early-childhood education field. I had the harmonica with me too. Isn't that interesting? I had separate dreams about those two things, and there I was simultaneously doing both. It's important for me to teach music because some of these kids growing up in their homes have never been exposed to music. It's amazing to me how music can bring such joy and enthusiasm to the classroom, embracing the social-emotional development of the child. They get more of a chance to express themselves in a dynamic way through music than they do sitting at their school desks. And adding the harmonica to the curriculum is very exciting for them and something they can approach on their own. It's so fun to reveal the sounds from the harmonica and the kind of music it can make. I hope they find their voice like I have found mine.

What's the best piece of advice you would give to beginners?

Relax and breathe in and out; get comfortable with learning to make sounds and notes. Then learn a melody. Listen to lots and lots of different harmonica players and genres.

What's the best piece of advice you would give to intermediates?

Practice with a band. Learn to play along with and accompany other players. And know when to play and when not to play.

What's the best piece of advice you would give to advanced players?

Play like a musician—make it sing; make it your own. Your mastery over the instrument is the music you make with it. And, contribute your knowledge and skills to others.

What has music done for you?

It's brought me relationships with people from all walks of life. I found that music was always the bridge to everything, a platform for relating to people on all different levels. Everybody comes together to hear a song they can relate to—it doesn't matter what demographic or socioeconomic background they're from. Music crosses the barriers in our society. I always thought, what a cool way to be able to reach and relate to the world in such a dynamic way that brings people together from everywhere with a positive impact.

Chapter 8

Lee Edwards:
The Yoda of the Harmonica

Lee Edwards, a Cardiff, South Wales, UK musician, is one of the world's few full-time professional harmonica teachers/coaches, and one of the early online harmonica teachers. His clientele, who come from twenty-three countries, take lessons either via Skype or in person in Cardiff. Known for his ability to motivate students of all levels, Edwards adapts each lesson to suit the particular person's needs and has opened the world of music and harmonica to hundreds of students. His clients consider him the Yoda of the harmonica world due to his passion for the theoretical, practical, philosophical, and psychological aspects of music.

At six years old, Edwards was encouraged by his primary school teacher to learn to play the recorder and piano. His love of music was so great that he began teaching himself how to play any instrument from which he could produce a sound, including the Magical Musical Thing, an electronic musical toy that included a songbook. Edwards soon learned to play all the songs in the book and then taught himself how to play the Thing with his feet. Two years later, he could read music and had added the xylophone and glockenspiel to his repertoire.

Upon graduation from high school, he trained as a graphic designer, then took on an apprenticeship as a mechanical engineer at a steelworks company. In order to earn more money, he became a pro wrestler while continuing his engineering apprenticeship. Edwards won both the European Middleweight Championship and the British Heavyweight Championship, but music was always essential to his life.

By the midnineties, he had gained experience on other instruments, including alto sax, various types of percussion, and of course, harmonica. Still a mechanical engineer, Edwards devoted his leisure time to playing harmonica, both in local bands and as a session player on projects from nursery rhymes to hip-hop. In 2003, the introverted Edwards chose to quit playing for live audiences and devoted his time to the practice and study of his craft. In 2005, he decided to teach harmonica full time and can be found at www.blowtheblues.com.

It sounds as if teaching keeps you very busy. Do you take on any other projects?

Certainly. I love to compose music, and I'm always willing to collaborate with others on projects that are interesting to me; but nothing compares to witnessing people develop as musicians in front of your eyes, knowing that you've helped it to happen.

You're a Welshman, but you teach harmonica, including American blues. What was your first exposure to American blues?

There aren't many styles of music that I don't enjoy, but blues, jazz, gospel, and anything that grew out of those, such as funk, R&B, soul, hip-hop, etc., have a stronger gravitational pull on me, although as a small boy I had no idea about labeling music or fitting it into categories. I just felt compelled to listen, move, and play the music that I liked.

When did you first take up harmonica, and why?

Up until 1995, I'd heard lots of harmonica in various recordings, but hadn't really HEARD it. Then, all of a sudden, I listened to "My Babe" for the first time, and something in my brain must have been switched on, because from that moment it became important to be able to play.

I had (and still own) an old Hohner Chromonica that belonged to my late grandfather, and I attempted to get it to sound the way that I'd heard the blues guys make it sound. After a few days, I was frustrated because I still wasn't getting the right sounds. I visited a musical instrument shop to ask for advice, and while browsing the harmonicas on display, I noticed one diatonic model called the Hohner Blues Harp. Because of the name, I thought, *This must be the one that the blues guys use to get "that" sound.*

I got home, and the big moment had finally arrived. I opened the case, removed the instrument, put it to my lips, and blew. I remember being disappointed that I didn't sound anything like Little Walter within an hour, and after realizing that hard work lay ahead, I rolled my sleeves up and got stuck in. I had a compilation of Sonny Boy II hits that I took with me everywhere for about three months solid, studying it to the exclusion of everything else and mimicking him as best I could. After buying more harmonicas in different keys and working at it for at least eight hours a day, I started to shape up very quickly.

How did you end up teaching harmonica?

I've never let what I did to make a living define me as a person. I may have previously been a steelworker and wrestler to pay my mortgage, but I've always been a musician first and foremost. In a moment of clarity, I decided to take the advice of many a steelworks colleague that had repeatedly said something along the lines of, "If I could do what you can do, I wouldn't be working here"; so I resigned from a life of grime and started building my own teaching business. It was a huge gamble, but I was determined to make it a success. I may never become a millionaire, but I get to pursue my passions while spending time with great people.

You're one of the very few full-time professional harmonica teachers—many others combine teaching with touring. You also teach each student differently. How do you judge each student's needs? Is it based on their playing or their personalities?

It's a little of both. There are certain foundational technical skills that every diatonic harmonica player needs to have, such as the ability to play clear and accurate single-note phrases, good tone production, and the skill to play and hold bends with accurate pitch. When I first sit with a student and hear them play, I always listen for signs of natural rhythmical skill, as I believe that to be of vital importance. When a student lacks internal rhythm or groove, I will heavily prioritize my teaching in favor of that.

Some students are analytical in nature, preferring to understand a concept theoretically first before applying it practically. Others prefer simply to sit and jam with me, to listen and copy what I do. Some are lazy, some are impatient, some are too easily distracted, some are too rigid in their thinking. My job is to nurture a student's positive traits and provide a counter to their negative ones as best I can to help them become a more balanced musician, while at the same time making sure that we have a good time with lots of laughter.

Did you have a teacher, or are you a self-taught harmonica player?

I believe that all learning is self-learning, and the teacher is merely a guide. A teacher can demonstrate, explain, and advise, but the students have to learn to accomplish the skills themselves. Let's use bending as an example. I could demonstrate it and I could explain it, but until the students experiment and eventually FEEL what it is like to play a bend themselves, all they have is theoretical knowledge of a technique that exists.

If there was somebody local with whom I could have taken lessons back in 1995, I would have; but there wasn't, so I had to be content with listening to recordings of Sonny Boy II, James Cotton, Little Walter, etc., extracting as much information as I could, and working hard to achieve the sound that I wanted. Later on, I did work through the *Paul Butterfield Teaches Blues Harmonica Master Class* book, which I thought was intimidating at first, but very rewarding.

What kind of songs/rhythms do you like to teach best? What do you like to teach least?

As long as the student is excited, I'm happy to explore all avenues. If forced to make a personal choice, I'd say that I'm more drawn to the funky side of things. A I-IV-V twelve-bar shuffle, although still satisfying, probably inspires me the least due to the repetition over the years.

Who do you suggest students listen to on harmonica to get better?

It's important to listen to what you like the sound of. When you're a beginner there are some players that you'll think are marvelous. Later on, as your ears develop and your skills increase, you may outgrow that particular player. Try not to see it as a betrayal and begin worrying about it, especially when others may accuse you of heresy. Accept it and move on to your next inspiration.

I think it's a good idea to not limit yourself to just harmonica players. A good melody is a good melody, regardless of the instrument it's played on, so figuring it out should help you tremendously.

Can a Skype lesson be as effective as a lesson in person?

Absolutely. The only difference is that due to the small delay experienced during the call, which is inherent in the technology, it is rarely feasible for both the student and teacher to be able to play to a backing track at the same time. However, if both parties have the same track and the student has a way to record the demonstrations of the teacher for future listening, it's no big deal to take it in turns.

What are some of the best bits of advice you could give to someone learning to play the harmonica?

Firstly, that they're not learning to play the harmonica. They're learning to play music and using the harmonica to do it. I like to think of it in this way: if you learn enough about music as a language with grammar, punctuation, etc., you can learn how to operate any instrument and express your music through it. For example, if you know how a minor pentatonic scale should sound and you have that in your head, you need only learn the mechanics of producing a sound on an instrument, whether it be harmonica, sax, trumpet, etc., and you'd be able to play that scale. The instrument is only a surrogate larynx; your brain is responsible for choosing what to say and when to say it.

Secondly, be patient. Building any set of skills takes effort and time. There are no quick fixes, so beware those who offer them. As long as you are consistent in your efforts, you'll always be better tomorrow than you are today.

Thirdly, listen to lots of music that you like. There's a difference between having music on in the background while you perform other deeds and giving the music your undivided attention with the goal of extracting as much essential information as possible so that you know every note, every beat, every chord change. Anybody who has the sense of hearing can hear, as it's a passive process. Listening requires thought and focus.

What do you tell students who think they're terrible and talk about giving up harmonica?

That frustration and self-doubt are always going to be part of the experience. They're unavoidable symptoms of an underlying cause. If you can figure out the cause and treat it appropriately, the symptoms will disappear. The most common cause is the lack of genuine effort. Imagine somebody who practices one particular thing for twenty minutes per week for six weeks. Progress will be slow; they'll get frustrated and say, "I've been working at this for six weeks." I'd say, "Six weeks have passed, but you've worked at it for two hours, and so the results aren't unexpected considering the level of investment." Each individual has the freedom to choose their level of investment and should manage their expectations accordingly.

How do you have students learn a new song? Tab it? Play it by ear?

In the same way that we all learn to talk before we learn to read, I prefer the play-it-by-ear approach as a primary foundation, supported by tab or sheet music only when necessary to jog the memory. Building the connection between the ears, the memory, and the instrument is essential, especially for those who desire to be improvisational players.

How do you get a student from beginner to intermediate, and eventually, to advanced level?

The fundamentals are always key, no matter what the level.

Posture, breathing, accuracy, pitch control, tone production, rhythm, scales, listening, practice habits, etc. Beginners are introduced to these ideas, and from that point onward, they will always provide the foundation on which the intermediate and advanced players continue to build. All levels utilize the same core skills, so it's a gradual and organic progression with no distinct boundaries. The main difference between the levels is really one of detail, subtlety, and nuance. Beginners have just enough ability to view and create a very low-resolution image of their musical world. The more advanced players, having sharpened their mental and physical skills, are able to view and create a more detailed, higher-resolution image very quickly. The beginner, at first, has to consciously think about the simplest of acts. The more advanced player, after spending enough time consciously thinking about those things, will earn their way to performing those acts unconsciously.

What brand of harmonicas do you play?

Since I play a variety of different styles of music and use multiple positions, I play Suzuki harmonicas for the standard range of keys, due to their equal-temperament tuning. I also like the ergonomics, hole spacing, and weight of them. For low-key harmonicas, I favor the Seydel Session Steel.

Who would you consider to be your greatest musical influences?

On harmonica: Little Walter, Sonny Boy II, Sonny Terry, Paul Butterfield, James Cotton, Junior Wells. All the usual suspects, really. I think Paul deLay was pretty special. Todd Parrott is probably my favorite contemporary player. Outside of harmonica, and narrowing the list down to a top ten: Louis Armstrong, Django Reinhardt, Ray Charles, B.B. King, Sidney Bechet, Fred Wesley, Maceo Parker, Miles Davis, the Beatles, Howlin' Wolf, and Dr. John.

Do you have any last words of encouragement for aspiring harmonica players?

If you have enough passion to maintain your interest through the frustrations and disappointments and are willing to work hard enough, you'll earn the good times. Reward doesn't come without sacrifice.

Chapter 9

Rick Estrin:
Legendary Showman

Photo courtesy of Joseph A. Rosen

Singer, songwriter, front man, and virtuoso blues harmonica player Rick Estrin has been compared to Little Walter, Cab Calloway, Louis Jordan, Willie Dixon, and Leiber and Stoller. Estrin is "a weird combination of jive talking carnival sideshow hustler and world-class musician, whose solos (diatonic or chromatic) are a marvel of pure creative joy, inventiveness, killer tone, and timing," says Richard Sleigh. "Rick Estrin is not only one of the most underrated harmonica players on the scene today, but is also a master songsmith, storyteller, and first-rate entertainer," adds Dennis Gruenling. Since 1976, Rick Estrin has performed around the world, originally as the front man for Little Charlie and the Nightcats, and now Rick Estrin and the Nightcats. The band tours nonstop, reinventing, redefining, and revolutionizing modern blues.

Born in San Francisco, early on Estrin listened to records of Jimmy Reed, Champion Jack Dupree, Mose Allison, Nina Simone, and others. As a teenager, he identified with the urban, African American culture surrounding him, and at fifteen, he purchased his first harmonica. By eighteen, Estrin sat in at black clubs around the city. At nineteen, he moved to Chicago and worked with South Side bluesmen Johnny Young, Eddie Taylor, Sam Lay, and Johnny Littlejohn before meeting and jamming with Muddy Waters. Muddy told Estrin, "You outta sight, boy! You got that sound, boy! You play like a man, boy!" Muddy wanted Estrin to go on the road with him, but because of a missed phone call, it didn't happen. Estrin eventually moved back to the Bay Area, met Charlie Baty, and formed Little Charlie and the Nightcats.

Three of Estrin's songs are on Grammy-nominated albums, and he has won three Blues Music Awards. Estrin is equally well-known for his inspirational video *Rick Estrin Reveals! Secrets, Subtleties, and Tricks of the Blues Harmonica*, a video which is more than a teaching video, one whose purpose is also to inspire players and teach them little tricks to give them more confidence on stage. "This video is essential for all who seek blues harmonica enlightenment," says Joe Filisko.

How did you happen to play harmonica?

There was a band that lived down the street from me in San Francisco, and they let me hang out. The house owner gave me a harmonica and told me to learn how to play it. I went into a room and didn't come out for a couple hours. While I was in that room, I decided, "I can do this." At that time in my life, I was kind of a lost soul, and I came out of there with a purpose.

Did the guy who gave you the harp teach you?

He didn't know how to play. I'm self-taught and learned from listening to records. I knew I wanted to be able to cause listeners to have that same feeling I had when I heard these other people who'd moved me.

Just three years later, you were playing in clubs. How often were you practicing?

It became my focus. I just played all day, every day.

Then what happened?

I was in this ghetto nightclub in San Francisco. I sat in on one song. At that time, it was highly unusual to see a white guy playing this kind of music—I was a novelty. They offered me a one-week job. A couple of guys took me under their wing, and one became a mentor to me. In 1970, I moved to Chicago and played with all the greats who were still around. It was a really great, vibrant scene.

You were in Chicago when you happened to jam with Muddy Waters. What happened?

I went to Teresa's in Chicago, where they had the most popular Monday-night blues in town. It was packed. That particular night, the band was Buddy Guy, Sammy Lawhorn, and Fred Below. The club was in a basement with a linoleum floor, no bandstand. Musicians sat on dinette chairs, and different people sat in: Louis Myers, Billy Boy Arnold—I met Junior Wells that night. I sat in, and Carey Bell came up to me and told me he was getting ready to quit Muddy. He invited me to come down to the Sutherland Hotel, a nice jazz nightclub on the South Side where they were starting to have blues. He said if I came down, I could sit in with Muddy, and if Muddy liked me, I could have the job.

I played, and it went well. I told Muddy I was thinking about going back to California, and he said, "Don't leave town for at least three weeks." He gave me his phone number, and I gave him the phone number where I was staying. But I left that place, and my phone number wasn't the same; I didn't have the nerve to call Muddy, so I just kept waiting around, and then went back to California. The next time I saw the bass player, he said, "Hey man, what happened to you? You lammed out. You were supposed to be with us."

In hindsight, it turned out fine, because considering the kind of nut I was those days, I didn't need Muddy Waters cosigning how cool I already thought I was. I probably would have gotten killed or killed somebody or done something really stupid. Instead, I had the opportunity to learn some lessons and get the gig with Little Charlie and wound up having a career.

In 2007, you made your video *Rick Estrin Reveals! Secrets, Subtleties, and Tricks of the Blues Harmonica*, unlike any other harp video ever made. What inspired you?

Well, I was a little panic-stricken because Little Charlie told me he was going to leave the band. I knew I needed to do something to educate people that my name isn't Charlie. All those years, I'd fronted Little Charlie and the Nightcats; he was the guitar player, but I was the front man. People routinely came up to me and said, "Hey, Charlie." I got sick of correcting people. I'd say, "Look, my name is Rick, Charlie is the guitar player." And they'd say, "Okay, Charlie." I gave up, but I knew I had to teach people my name.

For years, I'd had this idea about what would be a good approach to an instructional video. I'd never been a teacher, but I wanted a title that made it seem like I was giving away secrets, shortcuts, and ways to circumvent actually doing the work. When I learned how to play, no one would teach you anything, and the only instructional material out there was wrong. Since that time, there's an entire industry of harmonica instruction by some great guys.

What do you want people to get out of the video?

I want them to stay awake while they watch it. Also, I'd like them to begin to grasp that playing harmonica is about what works—it's not about licks. Licks only work within a particular context. I hope they'll start to listen to music in a linear way and appreciate the conversational aspect of how music works and what makes it effective.

How do you get your harp to sound like the blues?

First, you need to get the blues in your head. If you can't hear it, you'll never be able to play it. Listen to the stuff you want to play; the more you listen, the more you'll hear. Once you have it inside you, you'll be able to figure it out by making little adjustments to the way you're breathing and the way you're shaping your oral cavity.

You've got to feel the pocket; get loose, don't play stiff. Move. Find your own little dance, feel the space between the notes. Space is a part of the music too. One thing the harmonica has over most other instruments: you can get little vocal sounds out of it with your mouth and playing bends in conjunction with small hand movements. You can get so many sounds out of it.

And you can play the greatest and most difficult stuff to execute in the world, but if the groove isn't there, if it's not in the pocket, it's not going to be effective. Conversely, you could play the simplest thing, and if you put it in the right place and it feels good, then it also feels right to the listener. It doesn't have to be much. In my DVD, I use Jimmy Reed as an example: he couldn't play much technically, but he was about as cool as you could get as a blues artist. And listening isn't passive, it's an activity. Shut up and listen to the damn song.

When you're playing with other people, what should you listen for?

Listen to what they're doing so you can fit in. Listen to it as a whole and don't have too much of a preconceived idea of what you want to play. If you've been working on some little lick, don't try and superimpose it onto something where it doesn't really fit. If it doesn't feel right, it's not right.

What about breathing?

Playing the harmonica is playing music. It's not working music or the harmonica. It's not supposed to be difficult. The idea is, in playing blues especially, avoid labor. You don't want to work too hard. There was an interview with Little Walter in which he was talking about people who work too hard to play, how they're going to kill themselves just blowing, putting too much effort into it. He said, "What you do is fill the harp with air and navigate." That was his term for it. You need to be relaxed. You also want to get a focused tone and get a big sound, but you don't get that with muscle; you do it with compression and having that good feel with your mouth and tongue and using your hands and the mic to your advantage. It takes putting in time and also trial and error, but in the end, the effort should be minimal. If you're trying too hard, it's going to sound like you're trying too hard, and that's not what you want to sound like.

How about some phrasing tips?

Listen to other people who play in a way that you like, in a way that moves you. Listen to what they're doing and how they put things together and what makes it effective. Understand what you're hearing; follow it as a little musical story, and you'll see the value of how the phrasing works and how it doesn't work. Make it say what you want it to say to have the effect you want to have on the listener.

And soloing?

Phrasing is a big part of that. Even within a verse, contrast is important. On the harmonica, if you're playing traditional blues, maybe you don't have the same range of notes as some other instruments, but you have a huge range of sounds and tones and shapes and textures and things you can play to make it sound interesting. Build a solo that sounds like it's saying something.

How do you make your playing more conversational?

By listening and perceiving those elements in other people's playing and seeing what makes it sound like that. It's little, small differences. In the DVD, I talk about repetition and slight variations on that repetition, and then departures from that repetition. And sometimes, you make the departure from the repetition seem almost like a surprise. All that's where the conversational part is. If you hear it that way, you work toward playing it that way.

How do you learn the language of the blues?

Listen to the great people, the creators. Blues is African and African American music, so that's where you start listening. There are a few great players who are not African American, but they learned their lessons from the very greatest players. Go back and listen to Little Walter, Rice Miller, Big Walter, Sonny Boy Williamson, and if you listen with the same kind of dedication that some of the modern greats had when they were listening, you're going to hear something that nobody else heard. Then you're going to be able to latch on to and expound on and develop that little aspect. You're going to end up sounding like yourself, which is ultimately what I wanted to do. I wanted to have my own sound and my own voice as a harmonica player, but it's very rooted in the tradition.

I know you've shared many of your performance tricks on the DVD, but is there anything you can share here?

There are visual aspects to performance, and if you're just standing there like you're waiting for the bus, it's not going to be effective. I tell players to develop their little moves, not just to help them feel the rhythm, but also to give them something for people to look at as well. It's trial and error, and it's an individual thing, because stuff that works for me is not going to work the same way for somebody else. If you think you want to do something and you think you can feel it, you've got to work on it and practice it, live with it, internalize it, and then, when you're performing, let it happen and let it come out.

What's the real secret of the harp?

Keep it in your mouth. Listen to people that move you. Put in the time practicing and playing. Hopefully you love it enough so it's not strictly tedium. You listen and you play and you listen and you play, and the more you listen, the more you're going to hear. There's so much stuff out there available now that I think it's a little overwhelming. When I was starting, there was little available for the style I wanted to learn. You had to get the album *The Best of Little Walter*, which had twelve songs, and the album *The Best of Muddy Waters*, which had twelve songs, and there wasn't harmonica on all of those songs; and you had *Down and Out Blues* by Sonny Williamson. I kept mining these little treasures of blues art, going back and listening for the nuances and the details and really trying to figure out what makes this work and how am I going to make it say what I want it to say. Now, everything is available, including alternate takes, and there are too many licks to learn; the depth is easy to overlook.

There are guys who really know the instrument inside and out and are teaching and have developed lesson plans and ways of explaining what's supposed to be occurring in your body and inside your mouth that are beyond anything that I could have imagined. Nowadays, there are a lot of great players and great teachers, but the very best guys who ever played this stuff have been dead a long time. Go back to that stuff, listen past the low fidelity, and try to have the patience to make these discoveries on your own.

Chapter 10

Joe Filisko: Master of the Traditional Harmonica

Photo courtesy of Joe Filisko

Hohner calls master player, teacher, educator, researcher, historian, lecturer, player, and performer Joe Filisko "the world's foremost authority on the diatonic harmonica." Dennis Grueling says, "Joe Filisko is not only one of the most knowledgeable people on the planet when it comes to all things related to blues harmonica, but he is one of the best living traditional harmonica players."

Says Rick Estrin, "Joe's tone is simply otherworldly, and he basically invented harmonica customization, changing the world for harmonica players everywhere." Richard Sleigh adds, "In the harmonica world, Joe Filisko is basically the equivalent of a force of nature. He goes in by land, by air, and by sea, but he does most of the work away from the spotlight."

Filisko is a riveting performer and a master of tone and nuanced tongue-blocking rhythms. He has single-handedly introduced traditional harmonica styles to an entire new generation of players. His coveted custom harps are used by the world's elite diatonic players, including the Marine Band Thunderbird, the finest low-key diatonic instrument on the market, which Hohner created to Filisko's specifications for the distinctive conical Filisko-designed cover plates.

Since 2003, he has performed internationally as a duo with guitarist/vocalist Eric Noden, one of today's premier acoustic country blues and American roots music acts. Filisko has been named Harmonica Player of the Year by SPAH, performed at the induction of DeFord Bailey into the Country Music Hall of Fame, and is featured in five harmonica documentaries. He performs regularly in Chicago and teaches popular weekly classes at Chicago's Old Town School of Folk Music.

Who put you on your musical path?

A few high school friends and a cousin, who all played guitar, were the source of my initial inspiration. My first real musical mentor was my college music and guitar teacher.

Why did you choose the harp?

I heard the harp while listening to blues guitar and found myself endlessly fascinated. Once I picked it up, I couldn't take it out of my mouth: the sound, the size, and the lack of visualization have kept me amused and entertained.

Did you have a teacher, or are you self-taught?

I've learned immeasurable amounts of stuff from great players. I've also done hours of home-study listening and transcribing many of the greatest diatonic harmonica recordings known to exist. Having my own style may have accidentally happened, but my goal was to learn from the best players I could, whether they were living or just left a legacy of recordings.

How much did you practice to get where you are today?

It's really not possible to estimate that. When I was a young player, I certainly had my streaks of going at it all day long.

How do you master your technique?

I do lots of listening to the recordings of both the masters and to recordings of myself. When I think I have it down, I record myself and then make humbling comparisons to the original—back and forth and back and forth.

Is scales practice important? Do you practice scales?

Scales are important, but scales and technique don't necessarily equal music. My advice is to learn songs that incorporate the use of scales. After people have put some time in, they'll be able to play something musical. For folks who desire to play jazz, scales are probably a necessity. I practice scales to get myself over some obstacles in songs that I'm having trouble playing correctly.

You tongue-block almost everything. What do you think is the difference in sound between tongue-blocking and lip-pursing?

Tongue-blocking allows the quickest and easiest access to the biggest sounds you can make on the harmonica; lip-pursing tends to limit you to clean single notes, which, I believe, is the smallest sound the harmonica makes. There are some advantages to lip-pursing, but in my opinion, there are many more advantages to blocking. I believe that pursing is like the piano player closing his fingers into a fist and playing notes with only one extended finger. Tongue-blocking is like the piano player opening up all his fingers just above the keys. This allows for the quickest and easiest access to clean single notes, octaves, wide intervals, and chords—which make it easier for the player to get more sound out of the harp. The tongue does all the work, allowing the player to keep the harp deeper in the mouth, which tends to make the tone deeper and warmer.

How do you get that growling sound?

You probably mean the snoring pallet grind. It's really pretty easy to execute: just snore into and through the harp.

What tunings do you use?

I use the standard Richter tuning scheme for nearly everything that I do. I like the temperament to have the triads in perfect tune, and I'm grumpy if my octaves are not in tune.

What harps do you use?

I'm a Marine Band man. That includes the 1896, Crossover, and Thunderbird.

What microphones do you usually use?

In the studio, I usually record with either an RCA 44 or RCA 77. Playing live, I will use a Beta 58. My "go-to" mic for playing through an amp is an American DT5 giant chrome bullet. I'm also beginning to use one of Greg Heumann's Ultimate 545s with his Bulletizer option, along with an Astatic T3 upgraded by Matti Akseba in Finland.

Do you teach everyone the same or teach each person differently?

When I'm working with students who are part of an ongoing class, I usually treat the time like a five-to-seven-minute private lesson and encourage them to play. After getting a read, I will point out what I think their successes and new challenges are in a way that is informative to the others in the class. It is not difficult to identify something that the student *can't* do. The challenge lies in identifying and clearly explaining the specific thing that will best get them to the next level in their playing and music. That, with a little work, they can do.

Can you give some specific examples of your teaching method?

My goal as a teacher is to put students on a direct pathway to learning the technique and musical language possessed by the greatest harmonica masters who have ever played. To accomplish this, my method is four foundational pillars. The first is the overlooked importance of positioning the hands and body, allowing for a more relaxed ability to breathe.

Second is proper embouchure development. I've developed a method which helps students remove confusion and misunderstanding about tongue-blocking. It's important for the best tone and biggest sounds of the harp.

Third is proper active breathing and how to practice to build the necessary skills for high-level playing through more breath control.

Fourth is working on an appropriate repertoire for the student's skill set and musical maturity. On their own, most students will try and learn a song too advanced and beyond their skill set. My beginning and intermediate-level study songs offer students more blues repertoire options than ever before.

What's the best bit of advice you could give to someone learning to play the harmonica?

My ten-second advice is to be relaxed and learn to breathe through the harp. And for blues, when in doubt, *inhale*! My one-minute advice is to learn tongue-blocking, as the tongue is to the harp what the fingers are to other instruments. The tongue can create rhythm and punch, allow for octaves, and effortlessly introduce a chord. While it may be possible for some folks to play anything on the diatonic harmonica, the reality, in my opinion, is that most mortals should first develop a solid foundation of blues and simple two-chord songs before progressing beyond.

And intermediates?

Listen to great players as much as possible. Imitate if you can. Record yourself. Listen carefully to those recordings so you really know what you actually sound like and what the difference is between you and the great players.

And for advanced players?

If you want to grow, then you should transcribe music of the great players. If having your own style is your thing, then you should transcribe recordings of your own best playing and solos and work at better developing your ideas.

You are the expert on both the history and mastering the skills of the pre-war diatonic. How did that interest come about?

I was driven to decipher some of the magic and try and preserve some of the history. Back before amplification, players from the rural areas—at least the ones that recorded—consistently had more interest in getting that bigger and fuller sound out of the harp, a sound that leaves me in awe. How could something so small and unassuming sound so big and complex? Since there are lots of chords in this genre, it is a great starting place for beginners. If you can breathe, you can play. If you can breathe with rhythm, you can play music. I'm fascinated at how something so common could have been so misunderstood, misrepresented, and poorly documented.

The harmonica has been called "the blind man's instrument." What does that mean to you?

I understand it to mean that one's eyes don't guide them and are almost useless in trying to copy what other players are doing. Their tongue embodies their sense of touch, and ears take the place of their eyes.

How do you teach improvisation on the harmonica?

As a general rule, I don't. David Barrett is the best teacher I've ever encountered on this subject, and therefore I point folks his way to BluesHarmonica.com. He's made this topic his main teaching theme for twenty-plus years. Improvisation, in my opinion, at least in the beginning, is what happens when you can't remember what you wanted to play but act as calmly and confidently as possible while playing the next musical thing that pops into your head.

You have said that if it weren't for musical theory, you wouldn't be as accomplished. Can you explain that?

The music theory that I studied in college has been very helpful and given me a basic foundation of rules for music. Knowing theory, in my opinion, does not guarantee music; it just points you into the correct direction for obtaining it and makes you more aware of the danger zones.

You've said you often drop your right arm when you are playing to relax. When did you start doing that, and did you invent the technique?

I have been insisting more and more in classes and lessons that if students are not doing anything to enhance the sound with their hands, then they are better off benefitting from the more relaxed posture. A tense upper body interferes with the breathing process. Making your body breathe when *you* want it to as opposed to when *it* wants to will result in enough tension; add on to that a bad playing posture, and you are going to have extra challenges.

You have spoken of the "mystery of the blues." What do you mean by that?

I suppose the way that it has affected music across the globe; also, possibly, how mysterious it is that the harmonica can produce such a heavy, dark, and low-down blues sound. It always leaves me amazed. It is no surprise that the genre of blues music has more widely embraced the harmonica as an important instrument than any other genre of music.

You began working on your own harmonicas not long after you began playing them. How did that happen?

I like to know how and why things work when possible and practical. At my first SPAH, I saw Dick Gardner fearlessly disassemble a harmonica, and I thought that I could probably do that too, so I did. It was the first time any of the pros had actually witnessed somebody actually taking a serious interest in their instrument. Back in about 1995, the new harmonicas coming out of the factory were actually unplayable in terms of how bad the response was. The pros started calling me, and that's what started my full-time quest.

Did Hohner commission you to build the Thunderbird?

No, they used my old idea for the conical-shaped covers necessary on lower-key harps and were very kind to give me the credit. Very cool to actually have readily available such nicely made low tunings. I had been making and using them for many years before, but didn't want to start really writing and recording with them until they could be readily obtained. Fortunately, Dennis Gruenling forged ahead with them. I think that they are one of the most exciting things to happen to the harp in decades!

Now that you've created the Thunderbird, are you done or are you constantly thinking of new creations?

Mostly musical creations these days, along with teaching materials, adding to the catalog at www.filiskostore.com.

You are a master craftsman. What are the three most important things to learn in building a harp?

First, it must feel good in the hands and mouth. Second, it must be responsive, and third, it must be in tune.

What is the main difference for creating a harp for someone like Howard Levy and creating one for someone like Kim Wilson?

Understanding the playing styles and needs of the individual players. I believe that I have zeroed in on the requirements of the different playing styles now so that the creating is almost an automated process.

Do you find that more players these days favor diatonic or chromatic, and why?

Certainly the diatonic, because it's cheaper and easier to play. It requires less commitment to dazzle an audience.

How do you keep it interesting for yourself if you are performing the same songs in concert?

It just never seems to get boring. I guess the moral of the story is to be sure and write and record songs that you won't eventually hate, outgrow, or by which you'll be embarrassed.

How do you imbibe the instrument with that sense of magic?

Since the public has a pretty low standard of expectations of what the harmonica can do, it is often easy to appear magical to them. Especially with no hands!

When teaching, what's the most important thing you want your students to take away?

To always leave with the feeling that it is fun, they can be successful at doing it, and will always be faced with those endless challenges while always on the path of making the best music possible. I also try to make them aware of where they are gifted and challenged. Being self-aware of bad habits is a plus.

Which of all your diatonic playing talents are you most passionate about?

I'm most passionate about the one that allows me to play the right song, in the right way, at the right time. I also really like songs and grooves that play great on the tuning configuration and chords on the harp.

What do you still have left to do?

More teaching, especially beginner's workshops. I want to get more people playing the harmonica while having fun and making the kind of music that does not make them a public nuisance. I'm also gradually doing more in the prisons these days.

What has music done for you?

It often defines who I am.

Chapter 11

Jon Gindick:
Pioneer of the Jam Camp

Photo courtesy of Montgomery Pollack

A pioneer harmonica teacher and creator of harmonica jam camps, Jon Gindick has been writing songs, playing harp and guitar, singing, and giving blues harmonica lessons for more than forty years. In 1977, he self-published his first blues harmonica instruction book and built a successful mail-order business selling the book by advertising it in *Rolling Stone*.

In 1982, he self-published his second book, and in 1984, published *Country and Blues Harmonica for the Musically Hopeless*, which sold over 1.5 million copies through 2000. During the 1980s he ran "800 number" commercials on late-night cable stations and appeared on Home Shopping Network, where he taught the host to play the blues. He also made an instructional video with B.B. King.

In 2001, he started Blues Harmonica Jam Camps, harmonica-learning seminars held in hotels around the country, and also created *Cross Harp Songbook: Bluesify Your Melody*, a book which taught readers how to play melodies in the cross-harp style. An avid songwriter, Jon's award-winning CD, *When We Die, We All Come Back as Music*, a collection of ten original songs, won several awards and made its way onto the roots charts.

"Jon's music draws on so many sources: not just the country and urban blues harp masters who were his first inspiration, but torch singing, fast folk, big band swing, and a vein of New Age mysticism that challenges, inspires, and comforts in the face of a cold, hard world," says musician/professor Adam Gussow. "It goes without saying that Jon Gindick is a virtuoso harp player with beautiful tone and an ability to weave intoxicating melodies around the songs. His voice has some of the wry humor and rough edges of a Delbert McClinton. The two also share an ability to capture a story in a song. Gindick can break your heart with his crying harp."

So, what put you on your musical path? How old were you? What happened?

Neither of my parents played music, but we had Larry Adler albums in the house and an old Packard Bell console TV record player. I remember lying on the floor listening to Larry Adler, the great harmonica player, play Gershwin. I took trombone lessons in band and found that I was a lot better at improvising than I was at reading music. Then, in high school, I wanted to be Elvis Presley. My parents bought me a plastic guitar with a big picture of Elvis Presley and a hound dog on it, but my sister sat on it and broke it. Then came the Beatles and "Love Me Do." I was fifteen, working at the packing house in Visalia, loading fruit. I would pass the hours in the packing house playing the Beatles albums in my head. All my friends had a band, but I didn't know how to play anything, so I picked up a harmonica and struggled.

How old were you?

Sixteen. I struggled with it for three or four years. I did not know what cross harp was; I had absolutely no information. My friends didn't let me play in their band, but I was discovering Paul Butterfield and I was also listening to jug-band music like Jim Kweskin. I went to college during the folk-music rage, and that's where I learned to play second position in cross harp.

Did you have a teacher?

No, but by then I had three years into working on that instrument. My first harmonica was a double-sided Echo Harp, more appropriate to playing old folk songs than anything bluesy. When I went to UC Berkeley, where I transferred in my second year, there was a bona fide music scene and everyone went to Sproul Plaza to jam. It was heaven. People came from all over the world to play there.

I majored in sociology and psychology, but I really majored in playing music at Sproul Plaza and listening to the folk music. It was more than fifty years ago, but I heard a very good harmonica player, Will Scarlet. He had a harmonica that he had made; the covers were made out of wood. Another time, an old guy was sitting at a bench, playing by himself. It was Reverend Gary Davis. That was where I got hooked and learned to play. My first real career job around 1974 was teaching harmonica. I was the only guy I knew who gave harmonica lessons. I was twenty-five or twenty-six years old. I created a business. It was the only thing anyone ever really wanted from me. It continues to this day.

What kind of harmonica lessons were they? Were they blues?

It was in a context of getting the blues sound on the harmonica. I didn't know much more than my students, but I knew how to get the sound. And then I made up my own music theory, which I had no background in but was intuitively correct. It was the idea of creating and resolving musical tension to a beat. I taught people how to take the harp and create tension while teaching them to play single notes. That was my main music theory. Then I discovered there were certain notes that would always work, and I called them safe notes. It's elementary, but it's absolutely correct. I have discovered that for beginners, it's much easier to keep the theory stuff to a minimum, but to give them important concepts. That's what I learned from teaching. And in 1977, when I wrote my first book on playing the harmonica, *The Natural Blues and Country Western Harmonica*, it used those ideas.

Did the book come with a harmonica?

Only when I put it in *Rolling Stone* magazine and advertised it by mail order. It was a book, a Special 20 harmonica, and a cassette for $13.95. It did really well. Every time I'd run the ad, I would sell one hundred units. The New York publisher Music Sales Corporation distributed it to music stores, and to this day I have my books with them. It's almost forty years. They were fun to create. I really like page layouts, making sure there's lots of negative space in the page. I love illustrations that make the ideas simple and easily absorbed. I looked at making these books about harmonica as art, just like harmonica playing is an art. It wasn't just words; it was the whole physical thing of having a living, breathing book. Then I made other cassettes and pretty soon had an ongoing business of harmonica instruction.

And since then, how many other books have you written? Is it all just kind of updates of your original book?

I have written five or six books. And the CDs were just as involved as the books. Unfortunately, as the world has changed, books have become less profitable. I've let some go out of print. One which has not gone out of print is *Rock n' Blues Harmonica* book and CD, in which I use fiction to explain things. First published in 1984, the book has been updated three times, and it's on Amazon selling strong. It was the book that introduced Stone and the Cave Boys and used silly stories to try to make harmonica playing and music accessible.

In 1984, I hit my home run. A publishing company contacted me with the idea of me writing a book called *Country and Blues Harmonica for the Musically Hopeless*. I basically took what I'd written earlier in *The Natural Blues and Country Western Harmonica*, gave it a different voice, updated it, and did a cassette. They sold over a million and a half copies between 1984, when it was published, and 2000.

Then what happened?

The company was sold, and within a year they dropped the title, so something I'd come to depend on in a major way was suddenly gone. And after many, many sleepless nights, I started Blues Harmonica Jam Camp in 2000. That's the best thing I ever did.

Where was it? How did you end up at Clarksdale?

Well, first I did it in cities: in San Diego, Jacksonville, and Austin. I worked with really great people: Dennis Gruenling, Jason Ricci, Jimi Lee. It was a two-and-a-half-day seminar. In 2008, I did one in Clarksdale, Mississippi, and was amazed how many people came—around forty. I don't like hotels, and the economy changed, and I loved Clarksdale, so I took them all to Mississippi and did it three times a year at the Shack Up Inn. The Shack Up Inn is such a unique place—they call it the world's biggest man cave. Over time, I found the perfect team, and I really like having people with different strengths as musicians, and different strengths as teachers, and different approaches. It's almost like a band: bass player, lead guitar player, singer. This combination of people has really helped create the experience that we have.

Who are the permanent coaches, and what do they bring to the table?

"Hash Brown" (Brian Calway) is an expert in traditional blues on guitar and harmonica, as well as a phenomenal bandleader for our band and old-school harmonica player. R. J. Mischo is a huge student of blues music and just a great performer. I've never seen anybody who can direct an unrehearsed band with such inspired expertise. T. J. Klay, along with being the gentlest and most sweetly engaging soul on the planet, is just phenomenal in a Nashville folk and country style. He's been a professional musician since he was a teenager and is a great rack harmonica player as well. He knows all about musical harmony.

A great, great asset. Richard Sleigh is a fabulous harpist, guitarist, harmonica technician, and teacher. Cheryl Arena is one of the most powerful, passionate players around. She's a completely unique player who uses all the techniques to create a complete harmonica approach to the blues. She has become our singing teacher; she teaches people how to learn to sing, but also gets them to do these doo-wop songs and choruses and just getting turned on to the joy of singing. She is a highly talented and unrecognized singer, blues harp player, and one of the most powerful Chicago-style players you'll ever hear. She's also been very instrumental in getting women to play the harmonica and making women feel really welcome. Women are really our most serious students and learn the fastest.

Our band is passionate, imaginative, and compassionate, and they love the beginners. Every coach I have loves beginners and in no way condescends. They're just great communicators and lovers of music.

How many camps do you now have a year?

One a year, in September. Five days in the Delta. Still $995.

What's it like to be a student in your camp, for a beginner, an intermediate, and an advanced player?

I think that it changes as your week goes on. When people first come, they're very excited, and also nervous and scared. They're inspired, they wish they were better, they're working on the challenge and the song they're going to do on their last day. First-timers might be afraid of not being included, and end up making lifetime friends and having their musical urges confirmed and strengthened. We try to keep it challenging as our players get better and return. We keep coming up with new challenges and new things for them to work on, which is one reason we've pushed the singing and actual performing so much. We also teach song-writing and have created a lot of songwriters who now write songs. One guy, Steve Tuna, has won awards for songs, and he started writing them at the jam camp song-writing class.

What percentage of your students are returnees?

About 40 percent.

And your students go play at Ground Zero, Morgan Freeman's club?

Yes, the entire camp goes down to Ground Zero, and one person after another gets on stage for a twenty-four-hour bar cameo solo. The place loves it. Maybe thirty or forty harmonica players, and the band is playing a nice shuffle. Students are nervous about it and then they do it, and it's so much fun no matter how they sound, because they have an audience and people are dancing and cheering them on.

What is the Sonny Boy Club?

On Friday morning, jam campers caravan about ten miles down Highway 49 to the tiny, broken-down Mississippi town of Tutwiler to see Sonny Boy Williamson's countryside grave. Tutwiler is where Emmet Till's body was interred in the 1960s, and it's where W. C. Handy discovered a man playing guitar with a steel knife. The old train station could very well be the one Robert Johnson sang about. It's a boarded-up town with an average income of about twelve grand a year. What it does have is a great medical clinic for the locals and the Tutwiler Community Education Center, a large facility with various programs for Tutwiler's children, seniors, and families. To honor Sonny Boy and to give back, I created a charity called the Sonny Boy Music Club at the Tutwiler Community Education Center. For the last five or six years, experienced musicians have taught music to the children in the community. The program is financed by jam campers who've contributed. Anyone reading this should consider making a contribution, because every penny goes to supporting the program. Just visit www.Tutwilercenter.org.

When people come to jam camp, what do you want students to walk away with?

We get students to ask themselves, "What is my next level?" And then students decide for themselves what's the next thing to master on the instrument. People say it's so overwhelming, there's so much to learn, and I like to say, "If you do the easy things really well, you'll be a good harmonica player." And it's true. Do the easy things really well, and then let the music do the rest. But there's more than that. There's the sense of community and being included, creating space for other people, using the magic of music to enhance your life and enhance the lives of others, to learn how to feel and project joy when you make music, to learn when to play, which also means when not to play.

What now?

I ask myself that question every morning. I recently decided to reprint my book *Bluesify Your Melody* and intend to keep attending and contributing to SPAH. At home in Ventura, I enjoy performing with a band or solo, and as a teacher/YouTube guy, I keep busy. I want to keep the Sonny Boy Club strong and keep writing and performing. Jam camp has created a world of friends, new ones every day. Music-making is a wonderful way to live, to create community, and to keep growing—and I'm lucky that's what my life has been about.

Chapter 12

Dennis Gruenling: Jump Swing BadAss

Photo courtesy of Joseph A. Rosen

Dennis Gruenling, known for his huge sound and swinging, highly original harmonica style, is one of the world's most innovative harmonica blowers. He has single-handedly pioneered an entirely new harmonica sound and direction by combining the blues harp with swing/saxophone traditions and styles. His dynamic style draws inspiration not only from the great blues icons like Little Walter, but also from great jazz horn players like Lester Young and Illinois Jacquet. Gruenling has received international accolades by countless critics and musicians including, from Charlie Musselwhite, who said Dennis Gruenling's tone and phrasing is "as good as it gets," and named Gruenling one of his favorite harmonica players.

Growing up in Piscataway, New Jersey, and obsessed with music, Gruenling already had his own radio show by the time he was in high school. These days, he hosts a weekly radio show on WFDU, *Blues and the Bat*. He played harmonica in local blues bands and soon became a rising young star. In 1998, he formed his own "all-star" band, Dennis Gruenling and Jump Time (including the great saxophonist Joel Frahm). Gruenling has shared the stage with such greats as Pinetop Perkins, Snooky Pryor, John Mayall, and Southside Johnny and the Asbury Jukes. To date, he has released seven albums of his own and is getting ready to release the second Nick Moss Band featuring him on Alligator Records.

A pioneer for bringing low keys to the forefront of different blues styles, Gruenling is featured on the cover of Hohner's Crossover harmonica box. He was a Blues Music Award nominee 2018/17, won Best Instrumentalist for Harmonica for 2019, is a Sonic Junction Harmonica Instructor, and has been voted Best Modern Blues Harmonica Player three years in a row. He tours, teaches, and can be found at www.badassharmonica.com.

Why do you call your website BadAss Harmonica?

Well, honestly, I couldn't think of a good name that wasn't boring, generic, or silly. While trying to brainstorm, I had someone tell me I was a "badass on the harmonica," and I thought it was just interesting enough to use.

Dennis Gruenling: Jump Swing BadAss

What put you on your musical path?

My dad listened to a lot of country and western, back when country had some western sound to it—and I heard a lot of music just by being at home.

Why did you choose the harp?

I was offered a harp for Christmas one year from a family member, and thought, *Sure, why not?* because I had heard some rock 'n' roll musicians play harmonica once in a while.

Did you have a teacher, or are you self-taught?

I tried to take lessons early on, but never really had any real lessons. I am self-taught.

How did you learn? How much did you practice to get where you are today?

Listening is the biggest part—listening intently and focused. I started by trial and error, just trying to get a halfway decent sound out of the harp. Then I tried to get comfortable moving around with a clean sound and work on getting a decent tone. I started collecting records and imitating everything I could. During an intermediate period of my development, I practiced approximately eight to twelve hours a day for at least a year. I still practice, but that made a huge difference in my chops, my skills, my thought process, everything.

You play with such extraordinary feeling. How do you get that feeling?

The "feeling" is such a HUGE part of this music, its tradition and appeal. Again, a big part of it is listening to players that have that "X" factor. I listen to players that move me and try to learn from them. I also worked at understanding the language of music and how to use notes to express myself. That's a personal journey that, if taken, everyone needs to take in their own way. My vibrato was a technique developed from practice (like any other technique) as well as work on my breathing and tremolo. But the notes and scales and vibrato and tremolo are all parts of a means to an end for me . . . the end being expressing myself and making music.

How do you do what you do? How do you master that technique?

Practice, practice, practice. And practice the right stuff. I wasn't afraid to learn from my mistakes—that's why you make them in the first place, anyway! So I would work on something, try to get it right, listen back, work on it some more, and keep dissecting it until I knew I could get it down. After that, you can maybe start using it as part of how you make music and communicate.

What kind of rhythms/songs do you like to play best?

I like a lot of grooves, but some of my favorites are swing, double shuffles, rock 'n' roll, and a nice greasy, low-down Chicago shuffle.

Who do you listen to for inspiration?

A lot of musicians. Some harp players may be obvious—Little Walter, George "Harmonica" Smith, James Cotton, Big Walter, and Papa Lightfoot, as well as guys that are still around and at the top of the blues game like Rod Piazza, Kim Wilson, Rick Estrin, Steve Guyger, and Jim Liban. I also listen to so many horn players, in particular sax players. Lester Young is my favorite; he and clarinetist Pee Wee Russell are my two favorite musicians of all time. So many other sax players, though, like Illinois Jacquet, Willis Jackson, Gene Ammons, Paul Quinichette, Wardell Gray, Red Prysock, etc.

Is scales practice important?

Yes, scales are important, and I always hated practicing them! I do practice them, however. I'm the kind of musician who bores of that since it's another thing that is a means to an end. I've seen a lot of things going on in the harp world for the past twenty years, and some are really exciting. But regardless of what instrument you play and the type of music you are playing, remember that scales aren't music; they can just help you play and understand music better if you know how to use them.

What is your approach to harmony?

I tend to think harmonically like a swing horn player most of the time. It also depends on the style of song I am playing. Again, going back to my theory, everything you learn and practice should become part of how you think and play, but a musician should play to the song and in the moment for this kind of music.

In your opinion, what makes a good musician?

A good musician, regardless of musical style or instrument, will have some understanding of how to work with different rhythmic and melodic ideas, and will also know how to use his ear. For playing blues in particular, I think even more important than scales and technical chops is the "feel," "groove," and "expressiveness." These are intangible things which a good blues musician should be able to make seem tangible to the listener. As a soloist in this music, the space, the tone, and the phrasing are so important. These are also more of an art than a science. Whether they actually get the blues may be debatable, but robots don't play the blues well.

What's your favorite kind of blues?

I have many, but 1940s swing—bebop-influenced jump blues and post-war Chicago blues are probably my two favorites.

Do you practice daily?

I practice constantly. I think music. I always did, even as a kid, but I thought everyone did back then. When I practice now, many times it's in my head. I get ideas, improvise on ideas in my head without even having a harp in my mouth. But of course, I also practice physically with a harp, just not as much. Sometimes I practice new songs or ideas I'm working on, sometimes just improvisation or work on getting out of my comfort zone. I also divide my practice time between improvisation and new ideas/songs to work on.

You tongue-block everything. What do you think is the difference in sound between tongue-blocking and lip-pursing?

I don't technically tongue-block "everything," but more than 99 percent of what I play is tongue-blocked (sometimes on holes one or ten I will use my lips). The difference in "sound" is tremendous! For one thing, the tone you can get while tongue-blocking (correctly) will be fuller, rounder, and warmer than lip-pursing. It's not debatable, it's fact. Your embouchure and supporting air chamber are shaped and resonate differently, and that affects your sound and tone. The ONLY people I know that claim this to not be true are people who haven't worked at tongue-blocking or haven't been shown how to do it well.

Even known lip-pursers have a fuller tone when tongue-blocking. This is not to say you can't get a good sound when lipping, but regardless of how good it may sound, tongue-blocking will enhance it. On top of that, there are many effects and textures you can get on the harmonica while utilizing tongue-blocking techniques that will enhance the sound and depth of your playing. I started as a lip-purser like most players, but when I realized how much there is to gain from tongue-blocking, I immediately started working on it.

Who do you suggest students listen to in order to improve their playing?

If you want to be a good harmonica player, listen to good and great harmonica players. For blues harmonica, that list includes Little Walter, Big Walter, Sonny Boy I (John Lee Williamson), Sonny Boy II (Rice Miller), James Cotton, Junior Wells, George "Harmonica" Smith, and some others. But what and who you should listen to, to improve your playing will also be relative to where your ability is.

Sometimes a more contemporary player may seem more exciting or interesting, but it will be very hard to learn or understand what they are doing if you haven't built a foundation of the early masters and the techniques they used. All of the best playing nowadays is built upon the greats of the past.

When and how did you start teaching the blues harp?

After playing one and a half years, I started teaching locally and through the mail. I wasn't a great teacher, but I could play okay and sort of explain what I was doing.

Can an online/Skype lesson be as effective as a lesson in person?

I started teaching online over twelve years ago, even before Skype. With the right instructor, yes, a live, online lesson can be just as effective.

Do you teach everyone the same or teach each person differently?

I teach every student differently, not only because that is one of the biggest benefits of paying for "private" lessons, but everyone learns and hears and understands differently. Every teacher, regardless of what they teach, SHOULD teach each private student differently.

Can you give some specific examples of your teaching method?

I teach just about any technique, skill set, habit, or exercise relating to blues harmonica playing. I do have a set structure in mind for each student and lesson, but just as in performing, the beauty and magic is in the moment, and a live private lesson should be treated that way. A good instructor should not only know how to teach well, but should also know how to help each student utilize their strengths and build up out of their weaknesses.

What's the best bit of advice you could give to someone learning to play the harmonica?

Listen as part of your practice time, and remember that if you take the time to learn things correctly, THAT is the true shortcut to becoming good on your instrument.

How do you learn a new song?

Piece by piece. First, by listening to it over and over. Certain songs are tackled differently than others, but I always start by being as familiar as possible with it, then take it in pieces.

How do you make intermediate players better? What's the best piece of advice you can give them?

Make specific goals for yourself, and focus on them, in addition to just playing and utilizing your jamming skills. The better you get, the more work it takes to reach the next level.

And advanced players? What is the most important thing for them to learn?

Think longer-term goals. That is, if you want to progress. Branch out of your comfort zone and maybe even search out new influences that aren't the obvious ones.

What brand of harps do you use?

Hohner. I tried just about everything out there, and for me, nothing compares to a good Hohner Marine Band–style harp, and no other chromatics I have tried have better tone.

What tunings do you use?

Just standard Richter tuning. I also enjoy and have been using low-tuned diatonic harmonicas for years. I used to get them custom-made by Joe Filisko and Richard Sleigh. Now Hohner makes a whole line of low-tuned harps called Thunderbirds with Joe and me on the box.

What microphones do you usually use?

I collect, rebuild, and sell vintage bullet microphones, so only vintage microphones for me. There is a big difference, because they do not use parts that are anything like what they used to use in these microphones. In particular, I like crystal microphones like the Astatic JT-30 and Shure 9822.

And amp?

My main amp is a HarpKing. I have other vintage amps, mainly Fenders or Gibsons, but the HarpKing is the most versatile and harp-friendly amp I've ever played through, especially on stage.

What amp and mic do you recommend for a beginning player?

That partially depends on what style they want to play, and what amplifier they will use (if any). If they are interested in blues, a basic vintage Shure magnetic, I think, is a good choice. There are many more nuances and depth of tone in a good crystal or ceramic microphone, but they are more fragile, and it takes time to work on harp technique as well as amplified technique. The vintage

Shure magnetics are good all-around mics to get used to if you want to start playing this type of harp without worrying about minor abuse to the microphone.

You have a new album out. Can you talk about that?

In 2018, we released the first album with the Nick Moss Band featuring myself (*The High Cost Of Low Living*), and currently we are working on our second release together for Alligator Records. I've known Nick for over twenty years, and it's a pleasure to be working with him and his great band both on the road as well as in the studio. We both have a love for the same styles of blues, be it traditional Chicago blues, jump/swing blues, or good old-fashioned rock 'n' roll.

What has music done for you?

Music makes me feel like myself. It saved my life. It made the great moments better, made the tough times easier. Music helps me to make sense of this crazy world we live in and helps me keep the sanity that I have. Music has helped me meet many great friends along the way, and I hope to continue doing so!

Chapter 13

Adam Gussow:
The Blues Professor

Photo courtesy of Steve W. Likens

New York City–born Adam Gussow is a blues harper player, memoirist, and a professor of English and Southern studies at the University of Mississippi in Oxford with a specialty in blues literature and culture. Says Ronnie Shellist, "Adam Gussow has taken the diatonic harmonica to new heights with instrumental rock songs and originals. In the past, nobody had recorded such tunes on a ten-hole harmonica, but Adam proved that this little instrument was more than capable. His style reminds me more of an electric guitar and horn approach, but on the harmonica. That's why he's the professor."

Gussow began busking in Harlem in 1986 with Mississippi-born guitarist and one-man-band Sterling "Mr. Satan" Magee. Known as the duo Satan and Adam, they toured internationally, played the Chicago, Newport, and New Orleans Jazz Festivals, and released two albums on Flying Fish Record, including the W. C. Handy–nominated *Harlem Blues* and *Mother Mojo*. In 2009, Gussow transformed himself into a one-man amplified harp band and released two solo albums, played harp in the Big River touring company, and taught blues harmonica at the Guitar Study Center in New York. He has done workshops with noted blues harp player Ronnie Shellist. Gussow is the author of five books and initiated Hill Country Harmonica, a two-day harp intensive in Mississippi. In 2018, *Satan & Adam*, a documentary about the duo (twenty-three years in the making) premiered at the Tribeca Film Festival and won the Music City/Music Film Award at the Nashville Film Festival. Presently, Gussow runs the Modern Blues Harmonica channel on YouTube and offers digital-download video tutorials on his website, www.modernbluesharmonica.com. I caught up with him in Oxford, Mississippi.

You were exposed to music when you were how old?

When I was a kid, my dad collected jazz records, so there was a lot of music floating through the house. My mom played a little bit of piano, and in the elementary school band I briefly played clarinet and flutophone. I could play "Turkey in the Straw" on the piano. In 1974, when I was sixteen, I got my first harmonica and electric guitar at the same time.

How did you happen to get your first harmonica?

I decided I was going to learn to play "Whammer Jammer" by The J. Geils Band and decided to figure it out on my own. I went to the local mall and got a Hohner Marine Band, key of C, maybe A. I didn't know what key I needed. I bought Blackie Shackner's instruction booklet and Tony "Little Sun" Glover's book *Blues Harp*. I struggled to copy the songs and just jammed along.

Did you have a teacher, or are you self-taught?

I had a teacher ten years after that, but I was self-taught. I also played blues guitar, which was very important to my approach to harmonica. I was fascinated by blue notes, by the blue third, the bent notes. I discovered that harmonica and guitar worked in opposite ways when playing blues. With harmonica, you're using your mouth to pull the pitch down. And somehow, I taught myself how to bend. With guitar, I learned to bend by pushing up. You squeeze the minor third up toward a major third, whereas with blues you pull the major third down toward the minor third. That fascinated me, the fact that there were these two ways of getting the same kind of in-between pitch. Later on, I gave up guitar. I said, "There's too many good guitar players. There's not a lot of good harmonica players. I'll go further if I just force all my musicality into the harmonica." That's what I did.

How much did you practice to get to where you are today?

I didn't have a conscious practice system, I just jammed along for hours. I put on records and played along with Eric Clapton and B.B. King solos. A lot of my practice consisted of playing along with records by sax players. This was so incredibly important. Houston Person, Hank Crawford, and Maceo Parker. I just played along knowing no matter how closely I copied them, I was copying sax rather than harmonica, so I'd get something that didn't sound like someone else playing harmonica.

What was it like playing and touring as Satan and Adam?

I realized I was dealing with a genius-level kind of guitar player who had an incredibly strong groove. I could latch on to the groove and then begin to figure out what would work with him, which was its own kind of learning experience. Me, a twenty-eight-year-old white harp player playing on the streets in Harlem. The moment Mr. Satan and I hooked up and grooved together taught me something really important about what made for good music: we were making music with each other.

His groove wasn't the same as the Chicago blues groove, which taught me you can bring your music to a particular moment, but you have to actually listen and feel and connect with what's actually going on, what the other person's actually doing. He didn't tend to speed up; I tend to push. He would sort of swing hard, but lock it down completely. You can talk all you want about white and black or young and old, but we were together like a twelve-cylinder Duesenberg on all cylinders.

What did you learn from Mr. Satan?

He was about making everything beautiful, filled with this energy that needed to express itself in blues. Blues is about energy, expressing the euphoria or hardening you against the despair and keeping you moving, keeping you alive and kicking. Playing the harmonica is not just about playing the harmonica. There's so much else involved, the learning process.

What did you learn from Nat Riddles?

Everything. He was driving a cab which made a U-turn and came up next to me. I see this dark-skinned friendly guy. "Was that you playing?" he says. I said, "Yeah," and he goes, "It sounded good." And then he gets out of his car and takes out a harmonica case, opens it up on the trunk of his car. I'm standing there going, "What the heck?" Unlikely. But when you play harmonica walking down the street, stuff will happen. This is one of those ultimate moments when that happened.

He started to play and talk about Kim Wilson and Sugar Blue, who I'd never heard of. And he goes, "Oh, Sugar Blue, man, Sugar Blue is the best." He told me about Sugar Blue playing on the street and stopping people. He played and had some sounds that I'd never heard, which turned out was because I hadn't listened to certain players. I didn't know who John Lee Williamson was, the first Sonny Boy.

Nat said, number one, "You've got to learn how to tongue-block." His sounds were so extraordinary that I wanted to. So he pulled me in that direction. He was never a fast high-note player, but he said, "You've got to listen to Sugar Blue, that album called *Crossroads*, with Pontiac Blues." He goes, "You've got to get Big Walter Horton." I would watch him on the street do a particular lick, like on the F harp; he'd played a slow blues in the key of C, and he'd do a lick and then he'd repeat it. He really knew how to take his time and leave space. It's the leaving space that's so important. That's what phrasing is.

And there was one particular moment, the Fourth of July 1985, and Nat had the Fourth of July gig. He waited until the fireworks were over and the crowd started to come down the street, then he kicked the band into gear. He played the first song, an E blues shuffle, for forty-five minutes, until the place was packed. One song. What struck me was that you could do that—long solos that had a way of blossoming. Each chorus blossomed out of the chorus that came before. That really impressed me. The idea that when you make music, it's really about what's going on in the moment. It's not just about preestablished licks or a preestablished way of playing twelve bars. You're carrying on a conversation and you're extending it. Whatever you end up playing—the accidents or the improvisations—leads you to make other choices a little farther down the line in the course of an extended solo. He could endlessly invent out of some basic materials.

What do you encourage advanced players to do?

I'd encourage them to listen to really good blues harmonica playing or good harmonica playing and ask themselves to start listening for the spaces, and ask themselves why the person made the choice to leave that space. Part of what makes Kim Wilson really good is that he has unexpected durations. The durations that he holds notes for, the place where he leaves the space, but especially the durations, are not quite like anybody else's, just the way that Little Walter has a rhythmic concept that Wilson, of course, has expanded on and knows well, that involves a lot of things that aren't just kind of straight-up eighth notes and quarter notes. There's unexpected little rhythmic, little triplet-y things going on sometimes, and other sort of counterrhythms, or polyrhythms.

The rhythmic concept, the sort of sixteenth note or thirty-second note machine-gun thing, this is where it doesn't understand just how white it is, just how an African American musical approach differs from that. Think about Albert Collins, for example, as somebody for whom every note is angular edged and comes at an unexpected moment. That's not machine-gun stuff, and yet it's just about the most powerful blues guitar out there. Think about how different that is from a rock blues approach.

The best thing an advanced player can do would be to take a percussion class, and make sure that they really have the percussion, the sort of drumming side, down, the timekeeping side. What, as a player, is your rhythmic concept? It's one thing to think about pitches, but that's only part of how one might structure improvisation. I think you need to have a deeper rhythmic concept.

Have you ever had a period when you were uninspired, feeling as though you were playing the same riffs?

Yeah, absolutely, where you think you don't have anything to share.

What do you do?

I would say the best way of getting over that is to simplify radically. If I get a player who says, "I'm stuck, I'm losing interest," I try to get them using just three notes and get into a kind of funk rhythm; the second time, I do a little variation and set up a groove. Forget about changes, forget about complexity, radically simplify, and then start working little variations, and start listening for the things you could be doing.

That's the thing that gets me back into music right away, because it's a very musical thing to do, but it doesn't demand any conception of harmony. It's just about theme and variations and groove. Once you get those two things going, something simple that sounds nice, with a groove, and start varying it, then you get musical again.

I used to go through periods where I'd say I've fallen out of love with the harmonica. I've fallen out of love. And then I would think I just, you know, I don't have it. I don't have it. I think the answer is just keep living and think about what Mr. Satan used to say to me. He goes, "I won't be a slave to my guitar." So he would just put it down. Don't want to play? Put it down, and then you'll pick it up when you feel like playing. Very Zen, you know?

Do you ever get stage fright?

Oh, gosh, I got stage fright early on. I rarely get it now. I drank, for one thing, in order to not be nervous when I was playing in the jazz clubs in Harlem early in '86. I would sit at the table and put down two, three, four Heinekens, because when you've got that much adrenaline coursing through your bloodstream, you need to counterbalance it. The problem, of course, is if you get into a habit of doing that, and then the adrenaline starts to not be there, then you're just a drunk.

You can reframe, and think about who you're doing it for, expand something. You're not just immobilized inside your own anxiety, but say, "I'm here, I'm getting a chance to do this." I think looking on it as a gift, rather than "Oh my God, I'm afraid, it's being imposed on me." No, I chose to be here, and what a gift. The other thing is just keep doing it. It's basic psychotherapy; just keep walking into that situation, keep overloading, keep doing it, and then eventually it gets easier and you'll know what you're doing.

What kind of harps do you play? Are they customized?

I use a custom harp in certain keys, but there are other keys where I don't want it quite as bright. I started on Hohner Marine Bands, way back when I was sixteen, first one I got, and that's what I'm still playing. I'm an official endorser for Hohner, and while I've tried other harps, I have never consistently played another harp. I've tried other models of Hohner: the Special 20, Golden Melody, I've tried a couple Lee Oskars, tried Seydel. Eventually, I always came back to Marine Band. Ninety percent of my playing is in duo bands as an amplified harp player. I find the Hohner rich, mellow. I don't need custom harps. I actually think harmonica players benefit from having non-custom harps early on and developing chop strength. But if you're going to learn how to overblow, I think probably starting on a custom harp is the way to go, just because I think it's easier to lock them in. Then you can go back to non-custom harps.

What has music done for you?

It's given me an incredible sense of creative accomplishment, a sense of sharing something with somebody, of two people pulling the best out of each other. Because I had this extended partnership with an older African American musician in a black street context, it taught me an awful lot about race. There was a way in which the two of us functioned as racial healers, and I think it brought me much more deeply into that element of America. But I've also seen the world, a lot of Europe, Australia, and touring. I've been to forty-five of the fifty states. I would not have lived anything like a fully realized life without having picked up that harmonica early on.

Chapter 14

Filip Jers: The Swedish Harmonica Sensation

Photo courtesy of Filip Jers

Filip Jers, a cutting-edge jazz musician from Stockholm, Sweden, is one the most sought-out harmonica players in Europe. Only thirty-two years old, he has performed in many countries in Europe, Asia, Africa, and North America. European music critics call him the "Swedish Harmonica Sensation," as he plays every harmonica from chromatic to diatonic to bass. He also performs on jaw harp, guitar, and accordion, improvising and composing music and moving effortlessly between jazz, blues, folk and world music, pop, and classical music.

As a recording artists, Jers has been featured on more than thirty CDs and has been a guest musician to many other groups. He works regularly with the Filip Jers Quartet, Stockholm Lisboa Project, and Primus Motor. Jers has received twenty-two awards, including two golds from the World Harmonica Festival in Trossingen, Germany, the prestigious Björn J:son Lindh Scholarship, and most recently, Best Group (the Filip Jers Quartet Jazz Quartet) at the European Jazz Competition in Rotterdam, Netherlands.

Jers, who conducts workshops and harmonica master classes (www.filipjers.com), has taught at prestigious schools, including the Royal College of Music in Stockholm, the Malmö Academy of Music, and the Royal Danish Conservatory of Music in Copenhagen.

Were your parents musicians?

My father was a photographer by profession, but always played a lot of guitar and diatonic harmonica at home. He sprang from the sixties music tradition: blues, pop, folk blues. His father, a leather smith, also played traditional Swedish folk music, so I think, in a way, I'm third generation. My grandfather taught my father to play, and then my father taught me.

And on your mother's side?

My grandfather on my mother's side, a lumberjack, was also a musician who played piano, trumpet, and accordion. My uncle is also a musician. My mother plays piano once a year on Christmas Day.

When were you first exposed to music?

When I think of music, my first musical memory is the sound of harmonica. I started playing classical cello when I was seven, but my first music memory is when I was four or five and saw my father sitting in front of our house playing harmonica. Even though I started on classical cello, I was not so into music, but everyone said, "Maybe you should start an instrument," and I thought, *Yeah, why not?* It was like, maybe you should play football. It was not really my choice, but I played cello and learned how to use my hands and intonation and read music.

When I was thirteen, I started to play guitar and really fell in love with music. It was the Beatles, the blues, that sixties era. In that music, you heard lots of harmonica, so I thought maybe I should pick up the harmonica, because my father played it and I loved the sound. So my grandmother gave me a C diatonic blues harmonica when I was thirteen. But then it took a while to make it my main instrument because when I started high school, I was in a music program, and they weren't used to harmonica. They thought I should play other things as my main instrument, so I had lessons on guitar, keyboard, bass, and accordion.

So that's when you took up accordion?

I was playing guitar and bass in a high school band—we swapped instruments—and then I switched to harmonica, so we had a three-instrument combo. Around that time I was exposed to jazz harmonica because I heard Toots Thielemans do his thing. I was eighteen when I bought my first chromatic harmonica. Before, I'd been influenced by Howard Levy and the overblow and the chromatics of the diatonic harmonica. I think I was sixteen. It felt very natural from the beginning. I've noticed that some harmonica players who've played for thirty years suddenly find out you can play all the notes and it comes like a shock, but for me, it was nothing strange.

Did you have a teacher?

In Sweden, you just apply to the high school music program and have one lesson a week with a private teacher. I swapped instruments every year so I could get as many lessons possible. I had teachers on guitar, bass, accordion, piano, classical piano, and then bassoon. I had one harmonica teacher from whom I took maybe five harmonica lessons, and he said, "Now you know everything I know." But very early on, he taught me the art of customization on a harmonica.

You mentioned Toots. You spent time with him. What did you learn from him?

I met him four or five times, and he was just a very generous, humble old man. When I first met him, he sat there and said, "Can you play blues in C?" And I did that. And then he said, "Can you add sharp eleven?" And I did, and he said, "Good. Can you play sharp eleven and sharp nine?" And I did. And then he had me play the diminished scale and altered scale. It was kind of a test. And then he taught me why some keys work better than others and about improvisations, and he showed me diminished jazz runs. He was very down to earth and extremely generous. He also showed me some tricks on Duke Ellington's compositions. He said always play an Ellington song at every concert. It's very good for you; it's good for the music.

If you had no harmonica teacher, how did you learn, and how much did you practice to get where you are today?

My father taught me how to play a single note, how to tongue-block, how to bend notes, and all the harmonica basics. He showed me how to play Sonny Boy Williamson's "Help Me," and when I did that, he played guitar. And then he said, "Okay, you're done, don't practice anymore, because then you'll become better than me." But then I just practiced all the time. In 2002 or 2003 I was in Trossingen, Germany, at harmonica master classes with Steve Baker, Joe Filisko, Brendan Power, Carlos del Junco, and David Barrett. It was very life changing for me; I was having lessons with these great guys for a week. Then I went back two years later at eighteen and won both jazz diatonic and blues diatonic, the youngest winner ever. Only Carlos del Junco had won both genres before that.

Filip Jers: The Swedish Harmonica Sensation

In 2011, when you received your master's degree in fine arts in jazz from the Royal Academy, you were the first harmonica player ever to study there. How did that happen?

The Royal College of Music in Stockholm is one of the oldest music colleges in the world. After the World Harmonica Championships in 2005, I wanted to play harmonica full time and decided to apply for a music master's degree in harmonica. They didn't have a teacher for harmonica, so I told them to put me with the jazz saxophone players because we both play melodies and solos. I auditioned and was accepted. First, I did a three-year bachelor's program and then a two-year master's. It was an amazing school, with music performance as the main subject; you learned to become a full-time musician. I took lessons mainly from saxophone players, and also classical flute, folk music violin, and jazz piano, but I always played harmonica at every lesson. Then I took some lessons from a Finnish harmonica player, Jouko Kyhälä, who plays folk music and has good skills on Scandinavian styles of playing.

Speaking of styles of playing, how would you define your playing?

Interesting question. If I have to fill in a form, I would say I'm a jazz musician, because that's what I have practiced most in my life. But as my profession, I'm a musician that plays the harmonica. I play in many genres: I play jazz gigs, but also folk music, world music, and pop. And I add harmonica as a studio musician to anything that comes up.

What kind of songs do you like to play best? Do you have some favorites?

I love to play songs from the American songbook, the jazz standards, turning Swedish folk music into a more jazzy language.

Who do you listen to for inspiration?

If we just talk harmonica, Howard Levy is a big, big inspiration, as well as Toots Thielemans and Grégoire Maret, a modern jazz harmonica player who lives in New York. I also like classical harmonica players like Tommy Reilly and Larry Adler. I admit I am a harmonica nerd, but I also can listen to Mozart's Bassoon Concerto for an entire afternoon because I love the sound.

Do you play blues?

From time to time. I play mostly acoustic folk blues. Every summer, I play at the Blues Festival in Sweden with a Swedish guy who sings and plays guitar. And we play traditional blues songs. But it's often acoustic, not yet electrified harmonica, which I have not yet started. Everything takes time.

You also teach harmonica?

I was seventeen or eighteen when I had my first harmonica students or workshops for other harmonica players. Now, I don't teach on a regular basis, perhaps one or two students a month. But I love to do harmonica workshops as I have done at SPAH.

What is your practice method?

When I practice, I practice. I try to play every day—not all day, but every day. I often practice with a timer that I put on fifteen or thirty minutes a session. When the alarm beeps, I stop playing for one or two minutes. And then I go back. And that's given me a way to seriously focus in those fifteen minutes. If it's one p.m. and I have to do something at four, then I will play harmonica for three hours. Then I just go Facebook or eat or do other things. But when I work with the timer, I get so much more efficient in my way of focusing. I think focus is good for the brain and the body—kind of ergonomic. You won't create tension in the neck or get a stiff back or sore lips or anything by doing intervals, because you cannot sit too long. I exercise a lot; I do a great deal of yoga, and I'm a runner.

I also write a practice diary. I put the date, then, fifteen minutes I did a train imitation and then played scales for ten minutes, and then worked on some songs for thirty minutes. And then I repeat that or play two hours more. I'm kind of analytic.

What's the best bit of advice you could give to someone learning how to play the harmonica?

I would say to make your own musical mind map, because on harmonica you can never see what note you're playing with your eyes. You can on guitar or piano, but on harmonica, you have your own kind of guideline, and that can be very personal. You always know that this note feels this way or this note sounds this way, but now I know I'm in hole three because I can feel that I have two sides, two holes on my left, something like that. Harmonica is so personal that you try to become as aware as you can. And stay relaxed.

What's the best piece of advice you can give to an intermediate player?

I have a student, a blues harmonica player, who is very good. She wants to develop more third position or to play fourth position to get more minor sounds. She's already played the songs in second position with a lot of bending. So then we swap harmonicas and play the same music. I think that is healthy, because then you know how the music sounds, but you change harmonicas and change position and layout because it's nice to have a comfort zone and then just tension up the knowledge a bit.

What is the most important thing for advanced players to learn?

Just practice. That's no secret. It's just dedication.

Have you ever had a period when you were feeling uninspired? That you were playing the same riffs?

Absolutely. And then I play another instrument for two days, and then I go back to the harmonica with a lot of energy. And also, I try to change keys, just swap a key or to change the rhythm. If I'm used to playing, for instance, a blues shuffle, but I'm so bored with that, I try to play a waltz instead or make it like an Afro-Cuban kind of patter or play it as a ballad. I try to learn the songs I play on more instruments than harmonica. I cannot play them very intense—I'm not a guitar soloist in a band—but I know the chords, the melody, and I always try to do that early in the process of learning a song. I think it's good to have a higher kind of perspective.

What harp do you endorse?

I play Suzuki harmonicas, mostly Manjis and Olive. The nice thing about Suzukis is that all parts fit together so you can make your own bagel menu. I have a fabulous comb but Promaster cover. You can swap around a lot. I like these, introduced in 2009. Suzuki redesigned the reeds so they're longer and they respond better over bends and that kind of playing.

Do you tongue-block or lip-purse?

On chromatic, I try to do both because I noticed it really opens up the instrument a lot. And on chromatic, I also play Suzukis. I like the Sirius model a lot if you play the Toots way, but the classical way or the Bonfiglio way is more with tongue-blocking. They play on both sides of their mouth and make corner switches. You can play all these kinds of patterns more easily. Two days ago, I took a lesson from Robert Bonfiglio on tongue-blocking and corner-switching because I think it's good as a harmonica player to learn how to play as many embouchures as possible. It's good to be able to play lip-pursing, because then it's easier to move to incorporate bends to play chromatic on the diatonic. But then also to play tongue-blocking, swinging music, because that's what you do in the blues. I try to learn them all.

Do you have any new recordings?

I released a CD on www.filipjers.com, *Filip Jers Quartet Plays Swedish Folk*, last autumn with my jazz quartet. We play Swedish folk music in a jazzy way.

What has music done for you?

It has given me a life, and self-confidence, and opportunities to meet people and travel the world. I just enjoy being in the moment.

Chapter 15

Buzz Krantz:
The Santa Claus of the Blues

Photo courtesy of Grant Kessler

Ask anyone about Buzz Krantz, and they'll tell you what a great heart he has, that he has played Santa Claus for years, and why he is the ambassador for SPAH (Society for the Preservation and Advancement of the Harmonica). No one knows him better than his best friend, Joe Filisko, who first met him in 1990 when Krantz was president of Chicago's Windy City Club. "Being president of the club gave him credibility," says Filisko. "When we were going to SPAH, the guys his age were all playing chromatic style. He was one of few guys of that generation who was interested in blues, roots, and diatonic, and that gave him prestige, notoriety, and recognition from the old-school guys."

"Buzz is essential for what we do and who we are," says Paul Messinger. "You have to understand how the diatonic harp has become part of the harmonic landscape. Back in the day, it wasn't respected. Madcat and Buzz hung in there, and through their determination, brought it into a more equal part of the harp world; and that wasn't just because Joe Filisko started changing the instrument around—it couldn't have been done without Buzz's big heart. Buzz's essential goodness opened up people's minds. There was Madcap's great playing, Joe's great organization and ideas, but it was Buzz's heart that did it."

Winslow Yerxa is one of hundreds who proudly possess a T-shirt bearing a Buzz Krantz caricature and the legend *I'm a close personal friend of Buzz Krantz.* Says Yerxa, "The thing that really stands out about Buzz—aside from his appearance, which has often been described as 'biker Santa Claus'—is his outrageous sense of humor and how far he can push it without giving offense. One time he gave me an eight-by-ten glossy photo of himself inscribed to someone he considered 'inteligant.' In his trademark checkerboard shoes, Buzz has become an institution, the backbone of SPAH. I've watched him mellow over the years, seen his contemplative side grow stronger, and seen him don a T-shirt that looks like something from a biker club or heavy metal band, until you read the inscription: *Sons of Arthritis: Ibuprofen Chapter.*"

"Buzz Krantz is the definition of an ambassador to the harmonica community," says Jason Ricci. "I have hired him as a performer, teacher, and personality at every single event I have ever run. He is one of the most entertaining players out there and makes both professionals and newcomers feel welcome in any musical environment. It's really impossible to measure the impact he's had on the instrument and on blues music. He is a kind, selfless, talented performer and cheerleader for people, music, and the harmonica. We are very lucky to have him in our world."

"He's an extraordinary teacher," says Paul Davies. "The best quality Buzz has besides his ponytail is his sense of rhythm. You could set your clock by his rhythm and impeccable sense of timing. There are harp players who can blow circles around him, but no one can match his timing. He's an entertainer, a good harp player, an ambassador of the harmonica and of SPAH, and a legend who should be at SPAH every year."

"He has the biggest heart on earth," says Jerry Deall, "an incredible smile, a twinkle in his eye, he's very genuine and doesn't mince words, and he's not afraid to tell people he loves them. Besides being a very good harp player, he's a great guy to have a meal with because he's so much fun and exudes warmth."

Krantz might be known for his big heart, but he is also a talented musician who runs the world's largest harmonica jam sessions. He has won numerous awards, including the Best Harmonica Player in Illinois four years in a row, and three times NiteLife's Readers' Poll Best Musician for Harmonica, but the one of which he is most proud is the coveted Pete Peterson Special Lifetime Achievement Award from SPAH. He is a harp player who thrives on the magical connection between performer and audience.

What did you want to do as a kid?

I wanted to be a fireman, of course. No. I always wanted to be a musician. When I was in grammar school, an orchestra came in and played for the kids, and ever since then I always wanted to be a musician.

How did you start playing harmonica?

When I was about eleven, I had a friend who played

harmonica, and he gave me one and tried to get me to play. I didn't want it. Then when I was eighteen, another friend played harmonica and was pretty good, but I still didn't want it. When I was about nineteen years old, I saw Muddy Waters and James Cotton, and then I was hooked.

Are you self-taught?

I taught myself until I was in my forties. In 1989, I joined the Windy City Harmonica Club in Chicago. Al Fiore of the Harmonicats was a member and took me under his wing—that's when I started being serious about it. I met Joe Filisko in 1990, around the same time Joe and I went to our first SPAH. I haven't missed one since.

So, you were playing chromatic?

No. Diatonic, always. I never played chromatic. I love chromatic, but I love it when someone else plays it. When I play it, I don't like the sound that comes out of my mouth.

What was your first job when you were eighteen?

I had my first job when I was about eleven. I worked at a grocery store, and I had fifty jobs before I had my regular job.

And what was your regular job?

Airborne Express. I was there for thirty-eight years. But before that, I was a brewer. I worked at a strip show as a bouncer. I was a doorman, I sold candy, I worked in carnivals, and as an assistant manager for a Chicago theatre.

And you were playing harp all this time?

I got married fifty-five years ago, and I always played in the house or the bedroom or played with my friends, and I taught harmonica to other people. I really shouldn't have, because at that time I wasn't good enough. After I was married and probably in my thirties, Pam and I used to go to Old Town, where I worked as a bouncer. Old Town in Chicago is where all hippies were going. It's like Haight-Ashbury. I worked there so I could be there. I loved it there. I was a bouncer in a night club there for a few years, and that's when I started really playing, but I didn't really get good until I joined the Harmonica Club and met Al Fiore and all of the guys at the Harmonica Club in Chicago. Then I really got serious about it and met Joe Filisko and got even more serious about it. And then I went to SPAH and got even more serious about it. So, it wasn't just one day; it took many years.

Did Joe give you lessons?

No, I gave him lessons. The joke is that I taught him everything I know. I love Joe. Joe is my best friend. When I met Joe, I didn't like him. He was so quiet and laid-back—I was loud and outgoing. Totally different. Actually, he's been teaching me for years, but don't tell him.

Why not?

He's pretty much the opposite of me. I'm very gregarious and outgoing, and when I met him, he was very laid-back and very quiet, and I didn't understand that. He's come out a lot, and he's calmed me down, I suspect. Joe is a lot like my wife. My wife is a lot like Joe. She's very quiet. She doesn't like to be in the limelight. But I like to be.

I know, when performing, you love to say, "I'm not here just to entertain, but to have fun with all my close, personal friends." Where do you think that came from? You being in the limelight, being a jokester, an entertainer.

My father was like that. He sang with a band on the weekends. He was the life of the party and everybody loved him. I always thought that, luckily, I got that from him.

Was he alive at the time when you had that? Was he able to see it?

Well, I had it ever since I was born, yes, but he never saw me perform.

I understand that you used to play in biker bars.

I still do.

Do they get rowdy?

Biker people are really nice people, no matter what they do outside of the bar or whatever. I have been in places where I was absolutely terrified because of the kind of place it was or whatever, but I have never had any problems with anybody in a biker bar or in any bar. They are always very cordial to the band, and biker bars are the best place to stay sometimes because, like, these guys have pig roasts and they'll fill shopping bags for you. There was one bar I played in years ago, a really bad place. There were burglars, thieves, and robbers, and all kinds of stuff that hung out there, and I actually got mugged there once. But they always treated me nice. Bikers always protected us.

They must have loved you.

I am more of an entertainer. I am not the best harmonica player in the world, not even close. But I think I am a total package, an entertainer who might sing a little bit and play harp the best I can. I am just there to have a good time and make sure everybody around me does.

Do you play in a band now?

Yes. I play with a guy named J. B. Ritchie. He's a real bluesman.

And how often do you play?

I play a couple of times a week, and I also play in jams all the time. I don't like to play gigs so much anymore, because at seventy-six years old, I have a lot of problems. Mostly I'll play at jam sessions and have maybe ten, fifteen different bands that I play with, and they are all just friends of mine. I sit in, play two or three songs, sometimes the whole night. It depends on how I feel.

Do you practice?

Never.

But you teach?

Not in Chicago, no. I used to, and then it got to be too much of a hassle. I have a pension and I live comfortably; I don't need money, and I just go out and play. If I wanna play tonight, I know where to go. Every night of the week in Chicago, there's a blues band somewhere where I know the guy, so I can just go play. That's my practice.

When did you start playing Santa Claus?

About twenty years ago. A friend of mine across the street worked in food service for a big hotel. And every Sunday, he would have a brunch, and he had a Santa Claus. He always used to say to me, "Boy, Buzz, you'd make a great Santa Claus. If I need a Santa Claus, I'd call ya." Well, he calls me up on a Saturday night, and he says, "Tomorrow, I have a brunch, and my Santa Claus died today. How would you like to do it?" And I said, "Sure," because I love kids. I used to be a clown, I used to balloon animals. I went there and really loved it. I had such a good time I was a Santa Claus there for probably ten years. Then I started doing side jobs as Santa because he showed me how much money

I could make doing corporate stuff, and he started giving me jobs. Being a Santa Claus is one of the hardest things I have ever done in my life.

Why?

Because you have to put up with some really, really nasty people. But the hard part is the children. They are so wonderful and so much fun to be around; they keep you young. And then there are the people who are ill or have handicaps or are autistic, and you have to deal with them. And sometimes it's the most wonderful thing in the whole world, and sometimes it's so sad that you just cry.

I know you've haven't missed a SPAH conference since 1990 and that SPAH had a lot to do with you becoming a professional player.

Yeah. Because I learned so much from so many people, like Madcat and Joe Filisko, and people like that. It was just amazing. And, well, there are others too. Lots of people.

What's the best piece of advice that you can give to someone just learning to play the harmonica?

Don't do it as a business. You won't make any money. Do it because you love it.

What about intermediate players?

Go, have a good time. That's what music's all about. It's not a contest. It's fun. Go out and have a good time. Make the band sound better. That's what your job is.

And advanced players?

Same thing.

Have you ever had a period when you were uninspired, feeling as though you were playing the same riffs?

Always.

And what do you do?

There's always the glass ceiling, always. I listen to somebody else. Not necessarily harmonica players. I listen to music, and music eventually will come out in my playing. I mean, I can't play as fast as Jason Ricci, I can't play as well as Joe Filisko, but I am not afraid to get up and play with them, because I know I can play well enough to have fun with it.

What kind of harp do you play?

Joe Filisko makes the finest harmonicas in the world. I'm a Hohner endorsee.

What has music done for you?

That's a hard question. It's probably kept me alive. I've had a lot of sickness. I've got all kinds of heart problems, all kinds of sicknesses going on. Music keeps me alive. I love music. Music is my life.

Chapter 16

Howard Levy:
Jazz Harmonica Virtuoso

Photo courtesy of Yu Pei

Speaking about Howard Levy, Joe Filisko sums it up best: "Howard Levy is the man who can make the impossible seem effortless." Levy, who has been called the most radical single technical innovator in the history of the diatonic harmonica, is also known as the world's leading jazz harp virtuoso. A *Chicago*

Tribune reviewer attending a Levy concert noted, "Howard Levy unleashed more ideas in his opening solo than many musicians do in an entire set."

This two-time Grammy Award winner, innovative composer, superb pianist, recording artist, bandleader, teacher, producer, and Chicago resident is equally at home in jazz, classical music, rock, folk, Latin, and world music. He has been sought after by such artists as Kenny Loggins, Dolly Parton, and Paul Simon. Well known for his work with Béla Fleck and the Flecktones, Levy won a Grammy for "Life in Eleven," which he wrote with Fleck. His Concerto for Diatonic Harmonica and Orchestra is the first concerto for the diatonic harmonica using it as a fully chromatic instrument.

Born in Brooklyn, New York City, in 1951, Levy grew up listening to his parents' classical music, opera, and Broadway albums. At the age of eight, by his third piano lesson, he was improvising. For the next four years, he attended the Manhattan School of Music on weekends, studied classical piano and theory, and continued to improvise on the piano. At seventeen, he heard Chicago blues and decided he wanted to play the harmonica because he could bend notes, and unlike the piano, it was portable. His first blues harp cost $2.25. "I sounded terrible, until one day I bent a note, and that was sort of the first day of the rest of my life," Levy says.

Levy joined a blues band in Chicago and played piano and harmonica. Frustrated that he couldn't play all the notes on the harmonica, he discovered he could get some of those missing notes by bending the blow notes on the bottom of the harp. One day, a higher note popped out of a hole that just so happened to be one of the missing notes. Levy called it overblowing.

So, you basically invented overblowing?

I wouldn't say I invented it. There were people who did before, but nobody took it seriously. If you wanted to get all those other notes, you played the chromatic harmonica, which was designed to get those other notes. But you can't play blues on that instrument, and you can't really bend notes on it, either.

In 1970, when you were nineteen, you also discovered how to play the diatonic harmonica as a fully chromatic instrument. That was the overblowing?

Yes, playing the bends in tune, and the overblowing, and on the top of the harmonica, overdrawing, that's what I called it, because it was the same process but in reverse, trying to bend the draw note down on the top that doesn't bend. It's a combination of those different techniques that gives you a full three-octave chromatic scale.

You moved back to New York for a year and a half when you were twenty.

I played on the street and started teaching myself other instruments, too, whose sounds I loved: saxophone, flute, guitar, mandolin, violin, and percussion instruments. I think those instruments have helped my harmonica playing, because I close my eyes playing harmonica and visualize the piano keyboard, and that mental visualization has allowed me to start playing the harmonica the way that I do.

When did you start teaching?

Around 1973, when I was twenty-two. I've always shared what I know pretty openly with everybody; I don't have any secrets.

What do you teach?

Whatever a student wants to learn. I put out two harmonica instructional videos: *New Directions for Harmonica* on Homespun and *Out of the Box: Volume I* on my label, Balkan Samba. I wrote tunes in all twelve keys and played them all on a C harmonica. Then, I started my online harmonica school through Artist Works, which offers thirty-five teachers of all different styles of music and instruments. I'm the harmonica teacher. I teach at every level, from "Oh, Susanna" to really complicated jazz and classical pieces.

What's the best piece of advice you could give someone just learning how to play the harmonica?

Be patient. The harmonica doesn't give you much, and you can't see what you're doing. It's very frustrating that it's the only instrument that you can't use your eyes or hands to help you find a note. Spend a lot of time breathing through the instrument. Don't force it. Listen to a lot of blues harmonica players and imitate, because learning how to play the harmonica is like learning how to talk. You don't learn how to talk by reading a book on grammar. You learn how to talk by imitating people around you who were talking when you were a little kid.

Start on the diatonic harmonica with a lot of humility. Listen to tons of blues; if you're already a good musician playing another instrument, this is a huge help, because then you can figure out what notes you're actually playing. A lot of blues players don't know the notes that they're playing and they just play by feel, which works great if you're playing simple blues, because the Germans accidentally designed the world's greatest blues instrument—hilarious, but absolute fact.

If you want to get beyond just really simple blues, you have to learn what notes you're playing and become a musician the same way as people who play guitar, or piano, or saxophone. You have to know the names of the notes you're playing on those instruments. Often, diatonic harmonica players are not looked at with the greatest amount of respect by other instrumentalists, because a lot of us don't know what notes we're playing and we can't tell them what key we want to play a tune in.

Don't force the instrument to do anything. When people want to try to bend a note, they think that if they pull harder, they're going to get that note to bend, and that's not the case at all. It's just the resonance and position of your tongue inside of your mouth. That's why it helps to listen to really good players and imitate them. There are a lot of good books available, so people now have a really big edge over the way it was when I was growing up, where there was exactly one book, and most of the people who were really good players did not want to waste their time teaching some kid.

How do you make intermediate players better? What's the best piece of advice you can give them?

There are three divisions of levels at my school: basic, intermediate, and advanced. The way I separate it is, basic means that you don't know how to bend a note, and this level includes everything you can do with a harmonica without bending a note. And there's quite a bit you can do. Intermediate is where you can bend notes, do all the standard blues licks, and much more. My advice for intermediate players—which is basically people who can play blues and bend notes—is don't force things. Get a good tone. Let the instrument sing. Advanced is where you can do overblows and overdraws and play the instrument fully chromatically.

I think everyone should learn how to adjust the reeds on the harmonica, too. If you have a problem with the harmonica, don't be afraid to open it up. Learn how to tune your reeds; don't be afraid of the instrument, because when they used to cost two dollars, you could throw them out, but now they're a lot more expensive. You don't want to have to send a harmonica to somebody to fix it if one reed goes out of tune. You don't want to throw it away. You want to learn how to tune reeds—it's not that hard.

Now that 90 percent of harmonicas are put together with screws, it's a lot easier, because you can take the reed plates off the comb and you can get to those blow reeds much more easily. In the old days, you couldn't really tune the blow reeds very well. I still have trouble tuning blow reeds that are in the harmonica. I have to take the top reed plate off and tune them the same way I do the draw reeds. But you can tune and adjust.

Do you do your own tuning?

I do my own tuning, and I also replace my reeds. Replacing reeds is not anything I would recommend to people. It's very hard to do, because it involves tiny little parts, and I learned how to do it probably thirty years ago. It's like being a Swiss watchmaker. There are a few chromatic players who are watchmakers who do a lot of repair work on their chromatics, but there are a lot of websites that have information on how to do this. Tuning a harmonica is really not that hard, but replacing reeds is.

What brand of harmonicas do you play?

I've always preferred Hohners. I've tried all of them all; the Lee Oskar when it first came out, and then I tried Huangs, Suzukis, Seydels, and Herings. All of the harmonica companies have made certain models that I thought were pretty good, but Hohners, to me, are the only ones that feel like real harmonicas.

About twenty or twenty-five years ago, there was this kid named Joe Filisko who came up to me at a gig and introduced himself. He has turned out to be the Stradivarius of the diatonic harmonica world. He is the first person to come along and really make some improvements to the diatonic harmonica, to really enhance the performance of a diatonic. He started customizing harmonicas for me around 1993, and by 1995, that was all I was playing. About 95 percent of my harmonicas are those. They are a Marine Band replate, a special rock-maple-plywood comb, and Special 20 reed cover plates, which I like because they're closed on the end, and it gives you a mellower sound.

Before I played Joe's harmonicas for my jazzier stuff and in general, I played Hohner Golden Melodies, because those were actually the first diatonic harmonicas tuned to the tempered scale rather than just intonation or some compromised tuning. I'll still occasionally use a Hohner Special 20 or a Golden Melody. I really like some of the Crossovers and Thunderbird harmonicas, and I helped product-test those. Sometimes I'll try a Marine Band Deluxe and really like it, too.

Have you ever had a period when you were uninspired and feeling as though you were playing the same riffs?

Oh, sure. Everyone goes through that. The thing is that I always have the piano, which feeds my harmonica playing. I do most of my composing at the piano, so I always have a balance and a flow between those two instruments. I play the two of them together on a lot of things, so when you have me in a band, I'm almost like two people. Everyone goes through periods of relative flourishing and then relative stagnation, but at this point in my life, my musical life is so rich that it doesn't happen very often.

I feel so fortunate to be able to be in the place where I am now. I have a nice flow between composing, and teaching, and performing. There's this whole community of harmonica players all over the world who I'm in touch with through my harmonica school, and some of them come to visit me and take lessons. I really enjoy having people come from all over the world and giving them lessons at my house.

You've been improvising since you were a kid. Can you teach improvisation?

You can teach the tools of improvisation, and you can also loosen people up to have them improvise, mostly through singing. Improvisation depends on a relationship with the instrument, and also a relationship with your ear and your body.

Can you explain that, the relationship between your ear and your body?

If you can sing something, then you can play it. If you can't sing something, you can't play it. But instruments all give you something, so if you have some basic coordination, you can plop your fingers down on a piano and hit a bunch of notes, and go, wow, what's that? That's improvising. You have to be loose to improvise and take a flying leap into the unknown. You can be educated to a certain extent, but you don't want to learn too much terminology before you learn how to hear. Ear training is really, really important. All of us are born with different amounts of these abilities.

I have friends who have perfect pitch, and it seems like they've always been able to hear anything and play anything, and then other people have had to really, really, really work hard, and sound really great, but they had to work really hard to train their ears and apply that to playing.

What are the qualities that distinguish a professional musician from an amateur player?

You know that you're a musician if you try to do other things and you can't stand doing any of them. "Gee, I love music, and I'm working in this office, and I play music in my spare time." There's plenty of people like that. I joke around about this, but if you can't stand doing anything else, then you know you're a musician.

Being a professional means that you can't back off from this love that you have for the music, that you have to devote yourself to it and be willing to give your life to playing music. And of course, there's lots of different ways to be a professional musician: you can be a bandleader, a side man, an agent, a teacher—it's a huge field.

One of the things I think really builds a musician is touring. You also have to play a lot, be willing to practice a lot, play live a lot, sit down a lot and work on things, and compose, if that's the path you're taking. But, I think that going on the road, for somebody who wants to play well, that's the supreme test. That's what makes performers and differentiates the men from the boys: to go out on the road for a few months and have to play five, six, seven nights a week in all these different places, with various different surroundings and people paying an incredible amount of attention to you or not paying any attention to you, really crummy sound systems, great sound systems, terrible travel situations, awful hotels, beautiful hotels, whatever.

It's that level of commitment where you just commit your whole life to it, no matter what the situation is, you're going to always try to give your best performance, whether it's for four people or four thousand people.

Chapter 17

Delbert McClinton: At the Top of His Game

Photo courtesy of Joseph A. Rosen

Delbert McClinton, a blues rock and electric blues singer-songwriter, guitarist, harmonica player, and pianist, has been making music since 1962 as a sideman and since 1972 as a bandleader. Four of his albums have been number one on the US Blues chart, and McClinton has won three Grammy Awards. He has written songs recorded by the Blues Brothers, Buddy Guy, Emmylou Harris, Etta James, and Waylon Jennings, among others.

Brought up in Lubbock and influenced at a young age by Tejano, western swing, rhythm and blues, and war songs, McClinton developed a unique signature sound, making it virtually impossible to categorize his music. "Delbert will give you all the honky-tonk, heartache, blues, and kick-ass you'll ever need," says Bonnie Raitt. She adds, "He's also a great songwriter, harp player, bandleader, and entrepreneur, one of the most soulful, powerful singers I've ever heard, writes great songs, and plays killer harp. He's a national treasure."

Lyle Lovett says, "If we could all sing like we wanted to, we'd all sing like Delbert." Says Don Imus, "Delbert still sings his ass off. His phrasing is as good as Sinatra, and he is one of the best artists I have ever heard. He is a wonderful songwriter, his lyrics are clever, and yeah. He has God's gift for a voice."

How long have you been playing harp?

Since I was fifteen. Once every decade or so, I have disdain for the harmonica. In the early 1990s, I just put it away almost completely.

Why?

I just got tired of doing it. Then I came back to it, and it was a real pleasure again. Right now, I hate to play just regular blues and nothing more.

And what would something more be for you?

That would be to play punctuation and tracks that aren't blues. It's not disdain I have for the harmonica. I just cannot stand to hear bad harmonica players. Nothing is more depressing than to have to endure a substandard blues. It gets real old, real fast. I don't want to put my foot in my mouth; I've been doing this a long time, and I like a lot of different kinds of music. I am leaning more toward my jazz jams than anything and am loving it and having fun.

Were your parents musical?

No, my daddy had all the tap dance moves, and I've got the same rhythm he had. When I was a little kid, I thought, *Boy, that's really good.* And as I grew, I saw many people doing it. Tap dancers are so few, especially anymore. But my daddy had that rhythm, and it always excited me when he performed.

You were exposed to Hank Williams, and you picked up your first guitar at thirteen or fourteen.

I lived in a shotgun duplex with my family. I came home from school, opened the front door, and somebody was singing a Hank Williams song and playing a guitar. I rushed to where the sound was coming from. My older brother had a friend of his there, and he still had his oil-rig hat on, a long, tall guy. He was sitting on the floor singing some Hank Williams song. He had a little Martin guitar with a hole about the size of your fist; I later learnt he stepped on it when he was drunk, and I learned he had beer for breakfast. All these things I am soaking up, a thousand miles an hour. Just listening to him talk was like flying. I fell in love with his delivery, his sincerity, his blueship. I think that was the first time I ever took a step down this road, which was more than a mental thought, but an actual step. I had to do this.

And then a few years later you said "Honey Hush" by Big Joe Turner rocked your teenage world and that "Shake, Rattle, and Roll" was a further influence. Did that change your playing style?

No, it just enhanced it. Jump blues got me going; at that time, the music before it was called R&B. It was black music—roots music. And around 1951, it started getting national radio play other than on black stations. All of these things were happening at the same time: Chicago blues, Texas blues, Delta blues. Texas, for me, it was the Mexican rhythms that Doug Sahm was so good at playing, and then he turned around and played and sang the most badass blues. He was my first hero out of Texas who was alive, and he left a great legacy.

One day you were listening to KNOK radio and you heard Jimmy Reed's "Honest I Do," and that's when you got your first harmonica. So how old were you?

Well, I had harmonicas as a kid, but I got my first harmonica with the intent of playing blues music. There's a difference, because up until then, I was playing some songs like "Dixie." Anyway, it had been a plaything, and that day, it became an instrument for me.

So, what were you playing? Hohners?

Oh, yeah. Back then, that's just about all there was, unless you bought play harmonicas, which were pretend.

Were you self-taught?

Well, I was self-taught with the help of Jimmy Reed and Sonny Boy and Howlin' Wolf, the guys that I got to play with.

What did you learn from Jimmy Reed?

I learnt not to try to drink whiskey with two old black guys.

What did you learn from Big Walter Horton?

I learned that you gotta go deep. I learned that from all of them, but they all had their own voices.

What did you learn from Muddy?

I learned phrasing from Muddy. His rhythm and his voice were one thing, and that whole band became one thing when he was singing, and that's not an easy thing to do. And that's all before you realize he is one of the masters of the genre of music.

Your first record, which was a cover of Sonny Boy's "Wake Up, Baby," was the first white single to be played on Dallas/Fort Worth Black Radio Station. Did you think you were bound for fame after that cover?

I felt like I was bound for fame after everything we ever did.

And what happened?

Well, fame doesn't come like that. When I won that amateur contest in Cocoa Beach, Florida, at the age of seventeen, and that woman from Capitol Records came up and gave me her phone number and address and wanted me to send her a demo, I thought, *Shit, I am gone, man, this is it!* And every record I have done since then, I've felt this is the one. I heard a statement a long time ago: the definition of success is the ability to go from one failure to another without the loss of enthusiasm.

Your first band, the Mellow Fellows—what was that?

It was six guys who couldn't really play at all. Four of those guys were guitar players who couldn't play, and one of them was a saxophone player who couldn't play, and the other one was a drummer who was pretty good, but all he had was a snare drum and a ride cymbal.

On "Hey, Baby," you created the opening harp solo, and that song became number one in *Billboard* magazine. Did that start a whole new life for you? How?

At the time, we were just a bunch of young guys all out to change the world, and we were playing anywhere they'd let us for free. KFJZ was a radio station, and they played elevator music, but they had a recording studio and the engineer, Bob Sullivan, became one of my heroes. He recorded most of the early stuff that Hank Williams did, and he knew Hank Williams personally and everybody else that mattered in the business. Major Bill Smith would come down there and would find somebody to record. One night it was Bruce Channel, and Bruce and I hit it off immediately. We are still the best of friends. Bruce sat down and started playing "Hey, Baby," and I started playing that part. We recorded it no more than a couple of times because he knew it, it was his song. We knew the minute we cut it that it was a hit. It came out, and it was a worldwide number-one smash hit. In Europe, at soccer games, people sing that as their theme song.

When you heard Jerry Lee Lewis rock a version of "Crazy Arms," you said you learned that you could tear the tag off the pillow and not go to jail. What did you mean by that?

Well, I realized that Ray Price's way wasn't the only way you could do that song; you could do it and change it, and nobody would give a shit if you tore the tag off.

While in England when you were twenty-two, the then little-known Liverpool band, the Beatles, opened for you. What was that like?

You've got to put it in perspective: Beatles, Shmeatles. I didn't know who the hell they were.

What did you teach John Lennon about the harmonica?

I played it for him the way I did. You can't really show anybody anything. The best way to explain it is, it's kind of like masturbation—you fool around with it, you'll figure it out.

What kind of harmonicas do you play?

Hohner.

Are they customized?

No.

Are you a Hohner endorsee?

I used to be. I don't know if they even know who I am anymore.

Do you consider yourself a songwriter first, a singer second, and harp player third, or they are all equally important for you?

Well, I can play the harmonica. I don't play so much traditional blues harmonica as most people do. I like to do fills and punctuations with the harp, things that don't sound so gritty, because you can kind of wear gritty out. If I never hear another guitar player shredding, it'll be too soon. In fact, if I never heard another electric guitar, that would be fine. Last year, I had two guitar players out with me. My main guitar player had cancer and was going through treatment, and I had this other friend who'd played with me for years. Right before the gig, he had a moment where he didn't know what was going on and ended up spending the night at the hospital. We didn't have a guitar player, and I said, "Fuck it, we'll do it without it." One of the best shows we ever had. All the fucking guitar players were not in the way of the keyboard and the bass and the rhythm section and the horns. It was beautiful. It was wonderful, so I am not the least bit afraid of doing shows without a guitar player. That said, I love both of my guitar players and prefer to have them there.

What do you do to warm up before a gig?

Get drunk. I'm kidding, I can't drink anymore. Not that I ever did a lot, but I can't at all. I just try to deal with the whole fucking day in a hotel room. I like to stay at home these days. I don't give a shit about being on the road; they pay me to travel, not to play. Anyway, I don't really do anything except try to make sure that I rinse my head out, you know, with saline. Since I had heart surgery and quit chewing Nicorette gum and quit eating a lot of things, my voice has gotten twice as strong as it ever was. So, I don't do anything except go sing with it.

Did you have a heart attack four years ago?

No, I had a heart event. That's how it was explained to me. Damn near had a heart attack. We were setting up our equipment at this festival, and I started feeling really strange. I just got a feeling like nothing was right, not even the tips of my fingers. So, I said, "Guys, I think I need to go to the emergency room." Somebody called the EMS. Turned out I was 95 percent blocked in the main artery, and they did a triple bypass. Anyway, I went through all that melancholy feeling like I had been kicked out of my life and didn't know whether I could sing anymore. But when I came back and gave it a try, it was fucking great. The first show we did after I started back to work was amazing. I got really lucky with that one.

Has that changed your outlook on life?

Well, my outlook on life has been in flux all the time. So, whether it changed it—of course, I am sure it did. As to how, well, I'd rather go out and talk to the beautiful flowers that grow around my house and stay at home than do anything else. I've done my time, and so I do what I want to, and I work just enough to satisfy the Joneses.

Why did you start the Delbert McClinton Sandy Beaches Cruise, and what is it?

I played another cruise before that, two times, two years in a row, a rhythm and blues cruise. I love blues music, but I cannot stand mediocre blues music, and I heard a lot of it; that's not blues to me. So, I thought, *Shit, I can do a better job than this.* I can't imagine how we got the balls to do it, because it costs a million dollars to lease a ship. But we did it. Eventually, it started paying forward in sales. Now we have about 1,200 people. It holds a lot more, but there's no place on the ship big enough to hold everybody if you filled it up, so we filled it with what would be a good, workable amount of people. There are no assholes on our cruise. There's no low life. It's a bunch of wonderful people that come. It's the best therapy you can ever find.

What does music mean to you?

Music means everything to me. It's a song going on all the time. I am music, so to speak.

Chapter 18

Charlie McCoy: His First Harmonica Cost Fifty Cents and a Box Top

Photo courtesy of Pat McCoy

Country Music Hall of Famer Charlie McCoy has been a Nashville studio musician for fifty-seven years and has participated in more than fourteen thousand sessions. The seventy-seven-year-old has recorded forty-two solo albums with thirteen of his singles on *Billboard* country charts, served as music director for eighteen years for the syndicated TV series *Hee Haw*, and is a multi-instrumentalist whose instruments include harmonica, guitar, bass, mallet percussions (vibes, marimbas, bells, etc.), keyboard, trumpet, saxophone, tuba, vibraphone, and organ. McCoy has contributed to some of the most successful country, pop, and rock music recordings of the last six decades, including with Johnny Cash, Waylon Jennings, Loretta Lynn, Bob Dylan, Elvis, and Simon and Garfunkel.

Born in Oak Hill, West Virginia, McCoy's family lived next door to a musician who let young five-year-old Charlie strum his guitar. Later that year, the family moved to Fayetteville. Not long after, McCoy saw a comic book ad: "You can play harmonica in seven days or your money back, just fifty cents and a box top." (McCoy published an autobiography, *50 Cents and a Box Top*.)

Before long, McCoy could play all four songs on the instruction sheet, but the harmonica was short-lived. When in the third grade, his mother bought him a Harmony guitar from Montgomery Ward, which he still has today. By fourth grade, he was playing music with friends and won a talent show. At fifteen, his father bought him an electric guitar with a small amp. Soon, McCoy formed a rock 'n' roll band and played at school assemblies before forming his first real band, Charlie McCoy and the Agendas. It was the beginning of a lifelong love of music.

As a fifteen-year-old, you discovered Jimmy Reed. What happened?

I was fascinated. I said, "Oh my God, that's a harmonica and I've got one. I need to learn to do that." I had no clue that this instrument was used on the records, 'cause all I was hearing on the radio was guitar, guitar, guitar.

So you started learning harmonica à la Jimmy Reed?

I was lucky that I had a photographic memory, so I never

studied much in class. I had a lot of time on my hands to play music, especially as I was too little to play most sports.

You got to play with Chuck Berry. Were you playing harmonica and guitar?

Just guitar. I think I was in a coma the whole time. I was freaking out. We got to rehearsal, and I said, "Mr. Berry, what would you like me to do?" And he said, "Just be careful, son." I don't know how much I played. I think I was standing there with my mouth hanging open.

Did you learn anything from him?

Well, I was surprised he didn't play in open keys, the way it sounded to me. Then I realized, man, his fingers are so long, you know, he can play all this stuff in any key he wants to. He just confirmed to me that he was a fantastic guitar player.

You learned to play the double bass because you were in a new high school and guitar and harmonica didn't count as instruments in which you could major. Is it true you drew fret marks on the neck of the bass?

Yeah, there was no one to teach me, so I'd hit the note on the piano and go find it on the bass and draw a mark.

And how did you feel about the bass compared to the guitar?

I wasn't much interested in it.

Really? Because later you played bass on Bob Dylan's *John Wesley Harding*.

Well, later I got into electric bass. This was acoustic bass, and I was trying to play with a bow because I was in a high school orchestra. Bow playing didn't interest me much at that time. Later, I got into it.

On the *John Wesley Harding* album, your bass style was so unique, with tight, short bursts of melodic lines. How did that happen?

I was just using my Nashville studio training. I was fortunate to get to play with some of the greatest studio musicians in the world, like the Wrecking Crew, the Muscle Shoals guys, and Detroit Rhythm Section. They were expected to do three or four songs every three hours, songs they'd never heard, and that was the record. When I started, you couldn't fix something; you couldn't redo or overdub. It was direct to mono, direct to stereo, and these guys were great, just amazing. That was an education you couldn't buy. Plus, you were getting paid.

Do you still play bass?

Not a lot anymore, but I still love it and can still play. About all I do in session work anymore is harmonica and vibraphone.

Speaking of bass, when you were with Charlie McCoy and the Escorts, there was a song where you fretted the bass with your left hand and played trumpet at the same time, which you also did on Dylan's *Blonde on Blonde*. Can you explain that?

All right, I'm gonna kill that myth forever. I did not play bass and trumpet at the same time on a Bob Dylan record. I showed Dylan's organ player that I could do it on a session, but I never did it on Dylan's record. We had a bass player on *Blonde on Blonde*. I was just playing trumpet. But I saw a guy in a band do that once, and I figured out how to do it. You turn the bass up pretty loud and you just really thump on it with your left hand on the right place, the right string, and the right thread. The idea is to keep the bass and trumpet parts real simple. Riffs and things.

Charlie McCoy: His First Harmonica Cost Fifty Cents and a Box Top

When you were eighteen, Mel Tillis invited you to come to Nashville for a week.

He'd heard me sing and play. I think he'd been drinking a few beers too, but he walks up to me and says, "Boy, if you go to Nashville, I'll get you on record tomorrow." It was like showing a steak to a wolf. So the day after high school, I drive to Nashville and meet the boss man, Jim Denny, Mel Tillis' manager and music publisher who's also in the Country Music Hall of Fame. On Mel's word, Jimmy set up auditions with Chet Atkins and Owen Bradley. This is the beginning of my charmed career, because it all falls into place. I sing for Chet and play "Johnny Be Good," and he says, "Son, I think you're pretty good, but we don't do this kind of music here." So then I go to Owen Bradley, same comment. Here I am, I drove eight hundred miles and laid an egg, and he says, "I'm having a session this afternoon, would you like to come watch?" So I went back, and I watched thirteen-year-old Brenda Lee record "Sweet Nothings."

The first playback was like, "Oh my gosh, I want to do this." That changed my life forever, because my whole focus changed. I went back to Miami, dropped out of the university after a year, and moved to Nashville. A year passes, and Jim Denny calls and says, "I just got a call from Chet Atkins, he's recording an unknown female singer from Sweden named Ann-Margret and he wants you to play exactly what you played on the demo." So I already knew what to play. I thought I died and went to heaven. There was God, Chet Atkins; there were his disciples, the Nashville A-team musicians; there was his heavenly choir, the backup singers; and there was an angel, the twenty-year-old Ann-Margret. I ended up playing harmonica on the demo.

What happened next?

The bass player walked over to me, and he said, "Are you free Friday?" Hey, I was free the rest of my life. He said, "Come back to this studio, I'm recording Roy Orbison." I was a huge fan of

Roy Orbison. We did *Candy Man,* the record that really kicked my career and was a giant hit.

What was it like working with Roy Orbison?

He was great, very quiet, soft-spoken. A lot of people think about his singing, but what a songwriter he was. He wrote some of his songs almost like an opera. They start really tiny, and then build and build all the way to the end like a record, like *Running Scared,* a perfect example of how different he was as a writer. Incredible.

How did you start playing with Elvis?

He did most of his movie soundtracks in Nashville and had this group of musicians who worked every session with him. Then the movie company changed the dates of the recording, and so those guys were booked. It's an unwritten rule here; you don't cancel out on one artist to go play with another. So Scotty Moore, his lead guitar player, was given the task of booking an alternative band. I was on the band playing acoustic guitar. I never played harmonica with him until later on down the road when I did "Big Boss Man" and "High Heel Sneakers."

What was it like playing with Johnny Cash?

He was fantastic. The funny thing was the first time the producer's secretary called and said, "John wants to know if you can play harmonica like Bob Dylan." I said, "Well yes, I can." The reason I learned "Orange Blossom Special" was because of playing it on the Johnny Cash record.

What about Paul Simon?

He's one of those absolute hands-on people. The first session I did with him was "The Boxer," and I played bass harmonica. People said, "Man, that was a cool part you played." I said, "Hey,

Charlie McCoy: His First Harmonica Cost Fifty Cents and a Box Top

Paul Simon dictated every note." That's the way he worked. He's a genius, especially when you look at his body of work and the variety of styles in all those hits. At the time, he and Garfunkel were still together, and every time Garfunkel had a suggestion, it was almost like a recording; Simon said, "No, Arty, that won't work." Later, I worked with him on his first solo album. He did a song called "Papa Hobo," and we spent four hours on sixteen bars. Once again, he dictated the part and it was bass harmonica. Then he says, "I don't like this microphone." They go out and change the microphone, then we'd start up again. He said, "Now I don't like the part." So we go out and change the part. "I don't like this microphone either." I mean, this went on and on and on.

Did he have a legitimate reason?

No, it was just something he was looking for in his head that he wasn't hearing. We finally got it. It was great, but I was exhausted. Bass harmonica takes a lot more air than normal.

Are you self-taught on bass harmonica?

Yeah. I'm not like one of these guys that can play one of those trios; I just play effects.

Do you play chromatic also?

I own one. Couple of my own records I've played a couple songs, but it's not really my thing.

You play diatonic. What brand?

Hohner. I've been an endorsee for forty years of Hohner.

Customized?

I have some tunings, yeah, couple tunings I play, but as customized, no. Out of the box.

Do you consider the harmonica your primary instrument now?

Absolutely. I sound more like an individual, whereas with all the other instruments, I just sound like anybody else.

When you say you sound like an individual, is this a combination of your background of country and blues, and rhythm and soul?

It's a style that I developed, not only to do session work in Nashville, but to stay here. I dropped the blues stuff. When I came here, I played like Little Walter. I played like Jimmy Reed, which I still can. For a while it was a novelty. The record *Candy Man*, it's all blues. But I realized that if I'm going to stick around here, I've got to find something else. Number one, I cleaned up my tone. Number two, I started listening to fiddles and steel guitars and dobro and trying to play those licks like they were playing the country licks. Then I started playing melodies and playing behind singers, where my philosophy has always been less is more. It's worked out really well. The greatest compliment to me is if somebody says to me, "I know when it's you on the record." That's what every musician wants: their own style.

What's the best advice you could give to an intermediate harp player?

Stay out of the way of the singer. I hear young players who go play with a band, and all of a sudden, it's all about them. Hey, okay, I hear you, young guys, and they say, "What's your advice?" I said, "I would back off a little bit." I said, "I don't play that much on my own records." What I found is that if you're in a band, you get up and play with a band; they have a sound, man. If a guy gets up and plays without stopping, they're going to turn you way down.

What's the best advice you could give to an advanced harp player?

Try to figure out something that's your own. We've already had Little Walter, and he was the greatest. We've already had Toots Thielemans, and he was the greatest.

With the passing of so many great musicians, where do the blues and country go from here?

Well, harmonica runs in cycles. It's hot for a while, then it's not. We're in a down cycle now, especially in country music. Nobody hires me anymore. We call it the new country. A lot of the producers are younger than my grandchildren, and they either think you're dead or that you're retired. I don't much care for the records they're making here these days. I still get my share of session work. I'm going to end up with about forty sessions this year. I love to go in the studio with great musicians and play together. All my forty-two albums were recorded that way.

Needless to say, making CDs has become an expensive hobby because the internet killed the business. The only place you can sell is at concerts, and maybe some off your website.

What is your favorite kind of music to play?

Well, I'm partial to country, but I love blues. I love any music that's real. I don't care for rap or hip-hop; I want to hear music played by real people.

What is the future of the harp?

I have no idea, but there are some mighty good, young players around. Buddy Greene, Pt Gazell, Jelly Roll Johnson, Mike Caldwell—these guys are really good. I'll tell you that the instrument is in good shape right now.

What does music do for you?

It's not only given me a great career and made me a great living, but it's a happy place. When I'm playing music, I'm a happy camper.

Chapter 19

Charlie Musselwhite: King of the Blues

Photo courtesy of Joseph A. Rosen

Charlie Musselwhite's family considered it natural to play music in Kosciusko, Mississippi, where Charlie was born. His father played guitar and harmonica, and his mother played piano. When he was three, the family moved to Memphis, Tennessee. As a teenager, Musselwhite experienced the birth of rock 'n' roll.

Since that time, he has become an electric blues harp player and bandleader, has released over twenty albums, and has been a guest performer on many musicians' albums, such as Bonnie Raitt, the Blind Boys of Alabama, and Tom Waits.

Musselwhite was the inspiration for Dan Aykroyd's character in *The Blues Brothers*. He has won thirty-three Blues Music Awards, has been nominated for eleven Grammy Awards, and has won a Grammy for Best Blues Album for *Get Up!* with Ben Harper. He has received two Lifetime Achievement Awards and the Mississippi Governor's Award for Excellence in the Arts, has been inducted into the Blues Hall of Fame, and has won the Blues Music Award for Best Instrumentalist–Harmonicist many years in a row.

So, your family considered it natural to play music when you were in Kosciusko, Mississippi.

Well, nobody was a professional. They played in church, they played around the house. The closest to professional was an uncle who had a one-man band and was kind of a hobo. He told me he used to follow the harvest, and when people got paid, he'd be right there playing and getting tips.

When did you take up an instrument, and what was it?

There were always some harmonicas lying around the house; it was a common gift you'd get as a kid. When I was thirteen, I started collecting blues records, going around to used furniture stores to find old 78s and 45s. The main thing was that it said "blues" on it. The harmonica playing on those old 78s stood out and made me feel good to hear it. One day, I thought, *Well, you got some harmonicas. It feels good to listen to somebody else playing. I bet it feels even better to play your own blues.* I took my harmonica and went into the woods and started teaching myself how to play the blues, because I already had the blues.

At the same time, my dad gave me his guitar, so I was teaching myself guitar and harmonica, and eventually I got to know the street singers in downtown Memphis. I'd watch them, go home, and try to figure out how to play without seeing them play. Later, I got to know the real old-timers, especially Will Shade, who had a band called the Memphis Jug Band. He played harmonica and guitar and taught me both. He told me his mother taught him harmonica and she grew up in slavery. Also, there was Willie Borum, who showed me playing guitar with a harp on a rack. And Furry Lewis taught me slide guitar.

Did you want to be a professional musician?

I knew I wanted to see the world. It never occurred to me that anybody would be interested in listening to me play the blues, so I just assumed there was no way I could make a living doing that. When I went to Chicago, I discovered the blues all over town: Howlin' Wolf and Muddy Waters and Little Walter and Sonny Boy Williamson. I heard them all, but I wasn't asking to sit. I was happy just to be there. Coming from Memphis, I only knew how to drink, so I fit right in. They thought of me as just a fan because I'd request tunes. There were no kids my age, but I was eighteen and big for my age, so I could get in. After a while, this waitress told Muddy Waters, "You ought to hear Charlie play harmonica," because I'd played for her a few times. When Muddy found out I played, he insisted I sit in, which wasn't unusual 'cause people sat in with Muddy a lot. It was just unusual that a young white kid would be sitting in playing blues. So this got a lot of attention, and other musicians started offering me gigs. "They're going to pay me . . . to play the blues? I'm ready!" I had no responsibilities. I was young and out for a good time. And I had a heck of a good time.

When these other musicians asked you to play, did you get paid?

Oh, yeah, I got paid. Not a lot of money, but Robert Nighthawk was a guitar/slide guitar player and we'd play on Maxwell Street for tips, passing around a cigar box. And J. B. Hutto, another slide guitar player, and I toured a little bit together.

Didn't you and John Lee Hooker become great friends back then?

Yeah, he lived in Detroit but would come to Chicago to play, and I would do the same. We became immediate friends the first time we met. It was like meeting an old friend.

How did you finally create your own blues band?

I was doing different gigs in Chicago. If Johnny Young got the gig, it was a Johnny Young band. If I got the gig, it was a Charlie Musselwhite band, but the same band. Wherever you'd get the gig, you'd just call and see who you could get. No rehearsal. As time went by and I was learning all this stuff, somebody asked if I wanted to make an album.

And right after that album, *Stand Back! Here Comes Charlie Musselwhite's Southside Band 166*, you moved to San Francisco?

I went out to California to play some gigs. When the first album came out, I started getting calls from all around the country. Things were going so well in Chicago I didn't feel like going anywhere. But somebody offered me a month of work in the San Francisco area for really good money; I thought I'd go out there and come on back. But I don't think I was in California more than ten minutes and I knew I wasn't going back.

Was that during the flower children days? Weren't you kind of an exotic and gritty person compared to all these hippies?

I was staying on Haight Street and watching, which to me was better than going to the zoo. All these hippies with the tie-dyed clothes and purple hair; this guy comes up to me with the beads and the hair and says, "Hey man, are you Charlie Musselwhite?" I said, "Yeah." He says, "Man, you're weird." They're all into getting high and he says, "Man, you never got high, did you?" I said, "Man, what are you—I was taking acid from the Mafia when you were in diapers!" I liked the whole scene. They liked my playing and I always had good crowds, so I had a career. The West Coast didn't know about blues. A lot of young kids didn't even know where to go to hear the blues. I was playing in places like the Fillmore Auditorium, and they got to hear me.

You've said, "I only know one tune and I play it faster, slower, or I change the key, but it's just the one tune I've ever played in my life, it's all I know." Can you explain that?

That's just a way of saying style.

And what is style to you?

Well, when you hear somebody like you hear B.B. King, you can hear him play two or three notes and you know it's him. This is a tone, a sound, it's identifiable as you.

How do you get your tone?

I always assumed that blues was something you played as an expression from inside you. As I was teaching myself, I just played notes that sounded right to me. I'd play one note, then I'd think, *Okay, what's the next note I want to hear?* And I'd find that note. It's evolved like that. I couldn't help but have my own style, because I wasn't memorizing stuff off records. I was playing to the feeling and putting my own feeling in it.

Did you practice scales?

No, I never practiced scales so much. I taught myself how to read music and learned a little bit about theory and stuff like that.

Music in general is interesting to me, but improvising is the main thing I like. I really like phrasing.

What would you say is your strong suit of harp playing, besides tone and phrasing and what you come up with?

Survival. Staying alive is pretty number one.

Speaking of staying alive, in 1987, this little girl Jessica McClure was trapped in a well for over fifty-eight hours, and you said that inspired you to quit drinking. Why is that?

I'd already wanted to quit because I'd drink all day, every day. As time went by, it just didn't work anymore. I decided I had to stop. Finally, I only drank when I went to play because I had never been on a stage sober. I didn't like being in front of people, but if I was drinking, it was okay.

I heard about the little girl trapped in the well. They'd fed a microphone down and a speaker so they could communicate with her, and she was singing nursery rhymes to herself in the dark and cold. She even had a broken arm or a leg. I thought, compared to her, my problems didn't amount to a hill of beans. And I asked myself, *Why can't you get on the stage and do what you know perfectly well how to do, what's the problem?* I said a prayer for her; I wanted her to live. I didn't say I was going to quit drinking, I just said I'm not going to drink until they get her out of the well. That took three days, and when they got her out, I was out too.

You toured with Cyndi Lauper for two years. What was that like?

She's a wonderful human being and a great performer. I don't know anybody who works as hard as she does. She works hard on stage, and when she's not on stage she's doing voice lessons and taking yoga and doing things to help homeless kids. And as nice as she is, and as much as I love her, whoa, you do not want to cross that woman. She can be tough as nails in a second. But she and I always got along great.

You also jammed on stage with Mick Jagger. What was that like?

I was touring Australia and Mick was touring Australia with a band he put together, not the Rolling Stones. Mick had been playing in big arenas, and they'd been filming. They wanted to get some film in a club, so they wanted to come to this place where I was playing. It was supposed to be a secret, but that place was so packed that I was wearing glasses and they'd fog up just from the bodies in that room. But Mick was nice, and we jammed together a little and it was fun.

Who would you say has most influenced your playing?

My first influence might've been the late John Lee Williamson, the first Sonny Boy. I still listen to him. His playing might sound simple, but that's very deceptive. People also say Jimmy Reed's music is real simple, but I've never heard anybody nail the playing style. Even if they copy a solo note for note, they cannot nail the phrasing and the subtleties or the interior feel of the music.

You play chromatic, too?

Yes, I've recorded Jerome Kern's "Yesterdays" and "What's New" and "Harlem Nocturne."

Which do you prefer? Diatonic or chromatic?

Well, I'm more at home on the diatonic, but I love the chromatic. Maybe, someday I'll be as equally at home on the chromatic. All I need is time.

What kind of harps do you play?

I only play Seydel. I just think they're the best. I don't work on the reeds, they're ready to go. People sometimes give me a custom-made harmonica and say, "Try this. You're gonna love this!" It's okay, but it doesn't beat Seydel right out of the box. That's as good as it gets for me. The model I like is the 1847 with a wood comb and stainless-steel reeds.

Do you practice, or are you just too busy playing?

I practice sometimes. I want to make sure what I'm thinking translates to the harmonica the same way it does in my head, so I'll go over that. And sometimes I enjoy just playing along with a record or something, or looking for a new idea, just having fun.

Do you ever get stage fright?

That's why I used to drink. I don't get stage fright now. I spent so much time on the stage drunk to get over stage fright that by the time I quit drinking, I was used to getting on the stage.

Do you take chances on stage, or do you stick to the riffs you're comfortable with?

I'm always taking chances. Sometimes we'll do a tune we've never done before. I say, "Let's do a shuffle in B flat from the five." And I'll just try something out. The band are all such good players, I can depend on them and they're not going to fall apart. They're going to hold me up and let me play at my best. If you're improvising, you're always reaching for something new and taking chances constantly.

What's the best piece of advice you can give to someone learning to play the harp?

Play Seydel harmonicas. Buy all my records and learn all my solos. That's just a joke. What I would say is follow your heart. Play what you feel. And trust your heart. The music will take you where it wants to go, and that's where you want to go, too.

And what's the best piece of advice you can give to intermediate players?

Keep applying yourself. Don't be idle. And don't let it become a chore. Keep it fun and interesting. If you're having fun, you're learning. So just keep having fun.

And what's the most important advice you can give to advanced players?

It's time for them to retire. Just kidding. Have fun with what you love.

What has music done for you?

Music has taken me all around the world, again and again. I got to meet a lot of great characters and hear a lot of great music and experience a lot of different cultures. Music has provided me a rich life. I'm so lucky that the blues overtook me.

Chapter 20

Paul Oscher: Keeping It Real

Photo courtesy of Joseph A. Rosen

Paul Oscher is a legendary award-winning blues singer, songwriter, recording artist, and multi-instrumentalist who has recorded over twenty-four tracks with Muddy Walters, as well as dozens with other musicians. Oscher plays unadulterated, down-in-the-alley, gutbucket blues on harp, piano, and guitar. "He plays the soul I feel," said Muddy Waters. (Oscher was the first white musician ever to become a full-time member of a major black blues band—that of Muddy Waters.)

Oscher writes and plays his own music, and when he does play a blues classic, he puts his own stamp on it. "I always keep that low-down and lonesome feelin' I learned in Muddy Waters' band," says Oscher. "I like to keep it real and in the moment."

When you were twelve, your uncle gave you a Marine Band harmonica. Was your uncle a musician?

Yes, he played barrelhouse-style stride piano, but not blues. He put me on the musical path when he gave me that harp.

Jimmy Johnson, a Southern medicine show harp player who was passing by, taught you the rudiments of blues harmonica. How did that happen?

I delivered groceries to old folks after school. I was waiting outside the store for a delivery, and I was trying to learn the Marine Band harp. I was playing "Red River Valley" from the pamphlet that came with the harp. This black guy with a processed hairdo and gold teeth came out of the store and said, "Hey kid, let me see that whistle you got." I handed him the harp and he played *Wah wah wah wah* blues with great tone. The sounds coming from that little instrument blew my mind. Then he played a shuffle and tap-danced with it and turned the harp around like a clock still playing it. He was going to play it with his nose, but I stopped him. I had to learn what he was doing. He showed me how to choke the harp and bend the fourth hole. That's when I fell in love with the blues harmonica. About thirty-five years later, I figured out the clock trick, and I do it in my show sometimes.

How did you get so good so fast that by the time you were fifteen, you'd hooked up with guitarist/singer Little Jimmy Mae and begun playing professionally?

I played all the time, night and day, with a complete obsession and a love for the blues. I used to practice in the bathroom for the echo sound of the tiles.

How did you meet Jimmy Mae?

I was walking past a club called the Nite Cap, playing my harp; I'd gotten pretty good. A guy in the doorway said, "Hey kid, come in here and play that harp for the people." The club was all black people. He walked me to the bandstand and gave me a mic, and I played "Juke" and "Sad Hours." When I finished, they said, "Put your hands together for the little blue-eyed soul brother." The crowd went wild.

In the mid-1960s, you met Muddy Waters backstage at the Apollo Theatre.

There was a great blues show with Jimmy Reed, John Lee Hooker, Lightning Hopkins, Bobby Bland, T-Bone Walker, and Muddy Waters. I wasn't performing, but I was playing the harp at the back staircase. Muddy heard me playing. We hung with the band after the show at the Theresa Hotel, and he heard me some more and took my phone number.

In 1967, when Muddy came to New York without a harp player, you sat in with the band, playing "Baby Please Don't Go" and "Blow Winds Blow." How did you get to sit in with the band?

Big Walter was supposed to make the trip, but didn't show up at Muddy's house when they left Chicago. I sat in with the band, and after I played those songs, Muddy asked me if I could travel. Hell yeah! I met them the next day and got in the Volkswagen bus. Otis Spann was sitting there with his wife across from him. Drummer S. P. Leary was across from me, and Muddy's driver and valet, Bo, was at the wheel. Muddy, Snake, and Sammy were in a station wagon in front of us.

It says somewhere in Muddy's bio that when he first heard you, he described it as "Paul playing with Little Walter's amplified sound." But you were playing acoustically. Do you remember Muddy saying it?

I don't remember Muddy saying that, but that was the sound I had tried to get acoustically—very loud and fat tone.

When you were playing with Muddy, were you allowed to play what you wanted, or did Muddy tell you what to play?

Muddy never told you what to play, but if I played something he didn't like, he would cut his eyes at you and scratch his head, and you know you fucked up.

Did Muddy want you to play like James Cotton?

Yeah, Cotton or Little Walter. And he wanted Cotton to play like Walter until Cotton finally told him he could only play like Cotton.

What were the most important things you learned from the musicians in Muddy's band?

Tone, time, and phrasing. And how to be me. One time I was playing a Little Walter part on a song and I messed it up, and I said to Sammy Lawhorn, "Wow, I sure messed up that Walter solo," and Sammy said, "No you didn't, you was just playing Paul." I thought about it, and I never tried to play anybody's solo note for note after that.

Who would you say taught you the most about phrasing and timing?

Otis Spann. He would sit down with me at the piano till I got it right.

You lived in Muddy's house on the South Side of Chicago with Otis Spann, who taught you piano. How did that happen?

We both shared the basement. I had one room, and Spann and his wife, Lucille, had the other. The piano was in the middle room. Spann would play it all the time, and Lucille would sing. I never tried to play any licks exactly like Spann, but I know his timing and phrasing. I taught myself the piano. I first started by trying to play guitar and harp licks on the piano. Then Spann showed me a little simple left-hand stuff.

And you learned guitar simply by looking over the shoulders of Muddy and Sammy Lawhorn?

Pretty much. Of course, I was good enough on guitar when I started with Muddy to recognize what they were doing.

At the end of 1971, after five years, you left Muddy's band to form Brooklyn Slim?

Brooklyn Slim wasn't a band—it was a name I was using. Muddy sometimes called me Brooklyn Slim. I was playing in a bunch of no-name clubs, and I didn't want to associate "big-name" Paul Oscher with those kinds of gigs.

In 1976, you toured Europe with Louisiana Red, played with your own band in the New York area, and backed up Big Joe Turner, Doc Pomus, Victoria Spivey, Big Walter Horton, and Johnny Copeland. What did you learn from that?

The more you play with different musicians, the more you learn. I'm living in Austin now and have a quartet here; it's a steady gig, but my sidemen play behind lots of other artists and different styles of music. All the musicians are so good.

When did you develop your singing chops?

One night, the singer couldn't make the gig. We were playing in a black club in Bayside, Queens. I started singing, and nobody broke for the door or booed, so then I kept singing at least a few songs every night after that. This girl Deborah left me, then I really started singing and writing blues. She broke my heart.

Your harp playing has extraordinary tone. How do you get your tone?

Good sex! George Smith used to say drink milk (LOL).

You play diatonic, chromatic, and bass harp. Which of the three do you prefer?

I love them all equally.

Which of the three kinds is most difficult, and why?

Bass harmonica takes a lot of wind, and there's a large space to navigate. It's all blow notes. You can't breathe through the harp, and the reeds are unpredictable. They can choke on you if you blow too hard or too soft. I think diatonic is the hardest to play because you have to make all your notes and every harp is like a different-level reed.

As a blues guy, playing bass harp is unique. You're probably the only blues player to *record* using bass. When and why did you learn bass harp?

Because I had it, but I bought it in 1968 and didn't play it until 1994.

You play chromatic in a rack while playing guitar, another unique move. Is that as difficult as it seems?

The only difficult thing about that is the rack is so big you can't see where you are on the guitar when you look at the fret board. I used to fumble trying to find the guitar pickup switch and volume controls, but I just had them moved to the top of the guitar like a Les Paul that works great.

You have said, "The real gift of talent is not the ability to be able to play, it is the gift of the love you have for the music. That's what takes you over the hurdles." Do you ever get nervous on stage or feel you're giving a bad performance?

I always get nervous, but found that if I get to the gig closer to start time, I'm less nervous because I have less time to think about what could go wrong. I've found that you really need to stay in the zone when you're playing and not observe yourself while in the zone. Once that happens, you leave the zone; for instance, sometimes I surprise myself as I'm playing and say to myself, "Damn, that was cool." Well, it's downhill after that. Your concentration was broken by your ego.

You own a Hohner "Educator" harmonica. What makes it special?

That's a great harmonica, tuned like a Soloist, but that thing is tight and loud. It looks like a Navy Band.

Do you have other special harps?

The most special harp I have is a "hands-free" chromatic made by Vern Smith in California. You just move the mouthpiece with your mouth to make the sharps and flats like the slide on a chromatic.

Do you do any special tunings on your harps?

No. Now, speaking about special harps, you should know that the low-F harp was my idea. I asked Andy Paskas, a tech for Hohner, to make me a low-F harp from a Marine Band G harp. I wanted this because Muddy sang "Hoochie Coochie Man" in F sometimes and I wanted to play it in first position like I did when he sang in A or G. I played the low F for Mr. Hohner himself at the Hicksville factory, and he liked it and didn't realize a harp that low could be played that well; so about a year later, they came out with the low-F harp, and then later, other low harps followed. I never got credit or money for that idea.

You have played in concerts playing two different harps, alternating between a diatonic played through a section of PVC pipe, which serves as the *wah-wah*, and a mute, along with a larger chromatic. How do you do that?

I did that with an instrumental called "Alone with the Blues" on my album of the same name. That piece was in C, and I used a C 64 chromatic and a B flat super chromatic and a low-F harp, Melodica, and bass harp. It was funny in the studio because the helper had to hand me the Melodica and the bass harp when I needed them.

How do you develop breath control and tone?

I think you should never consciously think about breath control; just let it happen naturally, just like you would automatically take a deep breath after swimming underwater. To help with tone, first, get a clear vision of the tone you want; secondly, play long notes. Don't cut the notes off too short. Music can be like writing and leaving words out. Long tones also develop your wind. That's what I've heard trumpet and sax players say, but I never really tried to practice like that. I practiced by playing the same thing until I got it the way I wanted it. I never played scales or exercises. I always worked on something I wanted to use.

Do you practice anymore? If so, how and what?

I got a gig every week, so that's my practice. When I go on the road, I get more practice. The best practice you can get is playing before an audience. I do, however, try to figure out new ideas, and that's like practicing too.

Is your sense of rhythm innate? Can one learn a sense of rhythm?

I think you can learn anything, but it's like drawing—some people can draw naturally and some can't.

When you were learning to play blues, some harp players wouldn't share their licks. How did you learn your licks?

From records. You can watch a guitar player and you can see what he's doing, but you can't see what a harp player's doing; it's all in his mouth. James Cotton told me that when he wanted to see how Little Walter got that warble sound—if he was shaking the harp or shaking his head, something that could be observed. Little Walter turned his back on Cotton and said, "That's easy, it's like this," and played it, but Cotton couldn't see what he was doing.

Who is your all-time favorite harp player?

I don't have a favorite, but here are a few: Noah Lewis, John Lee Williamson, Forest City Joe, Rice Miller, James Cotton, Little Walter, Big Walter, Junior Wells, George Smith—they are all great.

What would be the best piece of advice you would give to someone learning to play the harmonica?

Listen to great blues harp players; practice and hang with musicians that are better than you. And always keep a harp in your pocket.

How do you make an intermediate player better? What is the best piece of advice you can give them?

Try to get your sound in your head, and keep fighting that harp until you've got it the way you like it.

What advice do you have for advanced players? What's the most important thing for them to learn?

Don't try to play better than your peers; just try to play better than yourself.

What has music done for you?

It's made me young when I'm old. I never grew up and I always loved music, so I never worked a day in my life. It was all pleasure. And it got me a whole bunch of beautiful women to get the blues about.

Chapter 21

Rupert Oysler :
Harmonica Zen Master

Rupert Oysler, president of Seydel USA, is also a harmonica player, technician, customizer, and one of the early proponents of embossing harmonica slots to make them play better. "He is a really a schooled and educated student of the instrument," says Greg Heumann, owner of BlowsMeAway Productions. "He's an outstanding player, but more importantly, he's a tireless ambassador for the harmonica through his work with SPAH and Seydel."

"Without Rupert, Seydel would never have anywhere near a presence in this country," says Paul Davies, SPAH's entertainment director. "He's also a low-tone master who is folky, gentle, never hard-edged, and a great musician with a very sensitive touch." Adds Pt Gazell, "He knew about the overblow technique many years before it became popular. He's really a schooled technician of the instrument."

"Rupert has been a great asset to all of us in the harmonica community for many years," says Todd Parrott. "He was one of the first to begin sharing information on how to customize and repair your own harmonicas by way of his DVDs, works that influenced many who went on to become great harmonica techs themselves. He introduced me to bending overblows when he demonstrated the technique on a phone conversation around 2001. His demo was the spark that ignited my pursuit and development of the style I play today."

"I believe his knowledge and ability to make harps play at their peak is one of the reasons he sounds so much better than the rest of us on super-low harps," says Jimi Lee. "His DVD *Harmonica Repair and Modification* offered many harmonica secrets and also revealed Rupert's hilarious dry sense of humor. To me, Rupert Oysler is a Harmonica Zen Master."

"Rupert Oysler is an outstanding harmonica player and repairman," says Charlie Musselwhite. "He's also an outstanding human being with great enthusiasm for life and a tremendous sense of humor, too. I always look forward to seeing Rupert because he's always uplifting to be around. He's definitely what I call one of the good guys! And he really is a really good guy. I'm all the better for knowing him."

Born and brought up in the suburbs of Chicago, Rupert Oysler began his musical career playing a toy harmonica at the age of eight. At Brown University, he studied art and thought he'd be an artist or a teacher, but preferred making music because sound happened in the present moment as opposed to a painting, which could only be observed. It was the days of the transistor radio, and at eighteen, Oysler taught himself cross harp by listening to records. By the time he graduated from Brown in 1970, he was getting paid to play in little coffee houses.

You participated in the folk music revival throughout the northeast US and taught yourself how to play guitar, banjo, and Dobro. Why?

I just loved the music, the sounds, loved the way that I felt listening to music and loved the process of making it.

You taught harp, banjo, guitar, and Dobro for the next ten years and developed a group teaching method that you presented at three colleges. What was that method?

I got involved with a banjo teacher who was really a trained classical bass player. I believe he played with the Knoxville Symphony, but he had been a banjo player as a kid all his life. He took this professional kind of musical training and developed a banjo method that was like the Suzuki-graded violin method—he based it on that. You learn something in lesson one, and then you build on that in lesson two, and then lesson three. By the end of ten weeks, you're playing some pretty decent stuff all built from phase one. I used that as a model to build a little harmonica course to teach people.

In the early eighties, you left full-time music to start a retail business and began training in the Alexander technique, a physical movement technique. Isn't that kind of farfetched from your musical world?

Absolutely. My life kind of represents multiple incarnations.

But you were also playing and recording in Nashville in the nineties.

Yes, I kept my toe in music.

You also became a pioneer in playing all the chromatic tones on a simple diatonic harp, and you won two awards at the International Harmonica Competition sponsored by Hohner. What was that?

They do an international competition in Germany, but they had it in Detroit one year. I participated in it.

When did you begin to experiment with repairing and improving harps?

In college, back in 1966, there was a guy who lived upstairs who had some chromatic harmonicas, and I didn't have a chromatic. I didn't even really know what one was, basically. He was doing things like dripping solder on the reeds to tune them, and he could replace a reed. This guy was kind of like the mad scientist and encouraged me to take apart little diatonic harps and try to make them work when they weren't working.

And you also decided to learn to read music?

Yes, some point in the eighties, because all my learning was based on tablature. It was certainly the easy way to teach harmonica. So I began training myself to read music with a chromatic harmonica, and I actually contacted Robert Bonfiglio at the Turtle Bay Music School in New York and took some lessons by cassette. That's what caused me to go to SPAH, to learn the background of so-called real music. There I was exposed to some chromatic players who worked on their own instruments. I met Jerry Murad and Pete Peterson, and Dick Gardner showed me stuff. I took some lessons from Stan Harper. The chromatic players all knew how to fix their harmonicas, knew how to make reeds out of bullet casings and springs out of diaper pins. I began to seriously learn about repair in the late eighties and early nineties.

What started you off on repair?

I was keeping my chromatics running. But then the whole diatonic movement of needing a better instrument to play these chromatic scales, from Howard Levy's influence, got a lot of us interested in "How do you create that, how do you make that happen?"

How did you end up at Seydel?

It's just like a dream come true, like a magic thing that happened. They are the oldest company and the youngest company. They had no awareness and no business whatsoever in the West. It was just a serendipitous thing. A guy in Germany was a harmonica player and salesman, and he had an online store. He was selling copies of my video, *Harmonica Repair and Modification*, so he knew me and he knew about Seydel. He actually became the first sales manager for Seydel when they got back in the game in 2005. He recommended that they use me to help get the West going, get the USA, get the North American market going. They contacted me, and I began working with them.

You said Seydel is the oldest harmonica manufacturer in the world and their instruments are still handmade in Germany. They're older than Hohner?

They started in business ten years before Hohner.

And their instruments are handmade?

I mean, they use machines, too, but it's a true handmaking process in that each instrument is handled by a person and tested and tuned.

What do you hope to do with Seydel in the future?

Every year, Seydel makes better and better instruments and improves what's already there. It's been a big help to the whole harmonica world in terms of some of the innovations we've come up with and some of the things that we create. I hope to continue in the vein of what we are doing and to get the awareness of our company more in the mainstream. I think we are really, really well-known now among harmonica lovers and people who are on the internet searching things out, but the average person still hasn't heard of us at all. Every day, I speak to somebody in an email or on the phone who says, "How come I never knew about you?" So it's really just to continue that growth of awareness that we are there.

Let's talk about your playing, because you're really an accomplished harmonica player yourself. Do you have a practice regimen?

It varies. There are times I have practiced for hours every day, and nowadays I try to at least get a few minutes in, but I don't play nearly as much as I want to. I work a lot of hours for Seydel, so my focus has not been on the playing in recent years. My life has been funny. There have been a lot of things that have come through and taken my focus away from playing, practicing, and from learning like I'd like to. Lately, basically, it's just to try to make sure that I put the harmonica in my mouth at least a few minutes every day. And I am really lucky, because I've been in a band with some guys for the last two years here in Asheville, so there's new material to learn, which keeps me going, and that's really good.

What's the best piece of advice you could give someone just learning to play the harmonica?

Just put the thing in your mouth and breathe. Just have a harmonica with you all the time, even if it needs to be a really cheap, crummy one, but have one there. Have one everywhere. Have one in your car if it's not in your pocket, and stick it in your mouth whenever there's ten seconds.

What the best advice you could give intermediate players?

It's still make sure the harmonica is in your mouth and begin to really fully listen to what's out there, to really fully listen to the sounds that are available. Whether it's on a harmonica or another instrument, just fully listen, begin to really hear what you love, and find a way to make those kinds of things come out of your harmonica.

And what about advanced players?

I am not sure I am advanced enough to give any advice. I think it's just a continuation of getting more and more accurate about what you are doing and what you want to do.

When you're playing on stage, have you ever had a period when you were uninspired and feeling as though you were playing the same riffs every time?

Almost all my playing is in a role of support, so I am listening to the other musicians and I am really living off of that. It's not so much where I am in charge of creating . . . so I don't know if I have really felt that way. I might have felt like I don't have enough skill here to really do what I want to do or something like that rather than I am playing the same thing. I tend not to play things that I have learned. I am playing something new every time.

What has music done for you?

Everything. Music is magic. It's something that, for the person doing it, creates some sort of a magic environment in your brain; it puts something out into the world which is just terrific, and it communicates on a nonverbal level something again that really needs to be communicated. It's like another dimension. It's a gift to the world.

Chapter 22

Todd Parrott:
Inspirational Virtuoso

Photo Courtesy of Keith Mitchell

Charlotte-based Todd Parrott, who has been playing harmonica for over thirty years, has been called one of the freshest, most innovative, and most proficient harp players today. "He's got it all: great chops, killer tone, speed, finesse, and impeccable taste," says Buddy Greene. "He plays with a sensibility and maturity and never sacrifices musicality for mere technique." Adam Gussow adds, "I think he's got the best chance of any harmonica player I've seen to cross over and become the public sound and image of what pure-D American blues harmonica is about: unamped, very little tongue-blocking, just straight-up, stand-at-the-mic-and-blow-the-hell-out-of-it stuff."

You were exposed to music when you were how old?

Growing up in the South, I was exposed to music as early as the womb. My mother was the piano player in our church up until I was born, so I was raised on loud, lively music from the very beginning. She tells me that when I was barely old enough to sit up, I could bounce in perfect time to the church music. My dad loved country music, my sisters were both great singers, and my brothers both played some guitar and loved old rock 'n' roll and blues. I wanted to learn to play trumpet in school, but my parents didn't think I would take it seriously and wouldn't spend the money. So the harmonica put me on the path of actually playing music.

What is your earliest music-related memory?

Listening to 8-tracks as a child on road trips to the beach and listening to records at home. I'm the youngest of five kids, so I was inevitably exposed to their varying styles of music. I was also fascinated with the drums, loved to watch the church drummer and loved the crash of the cymbals. My brother-in-law gave me a tom and some drumsticks, and I made up beats and rhythms and pretended to be the church drummer.

And when were you first exposed to the harmonica?

As a kid, an evangelist visited our church. He whipped out a harmonica and started to play. I was amazed and was determined to learn to play the instrument. On the last night of the services, I bought a harmonica from him—against my mother's wishes, I might add. The other kids laughed and teased me, but the harmonica stuck with me. I'm still playing harmonica.

What styles of music do you enjoy the most?

Any style, as long as it's truly musical. I appreciate creative chord progressions, funkiness, soulfulness, and rhythms . . . in other words, the song has to move me in some way. Some gospel styles, especially black gospel, possess all of these elements. For the last several years, I've tried to adapt my harmonica playing to various styles of music, which forces me to be creative and find other note possibilities than those associated with country and blues. I also love certain styles of jazz, though I'm not yet a proficient jazz player.

Did you have a teacher, or are you self-taught?

I've never had a formal music lesson. I listened to records and tapes for hours growing up, playing along on the harmonica and the piano, trying to figure out the chord progressions.

How much time did you spend practicing when you first began? And has this changed over the years?

In the early days, I would practice for literally hours every day, listening to other harmonica players and rewinding the cassette over and over until I'd mastered their licks. I never really thought of it as practice. I was just having fun with my newfound love of the harmonica. I do make it a point to play every day (even sometimes with one hand while driving down the road). Not only is this important for staying musically fit, but many times new ideas and licks appear out of the blue, and when this happens, I try and immediately record these ideas so I won't forget them.

How would you describe your practice routine? And how important is scales practice to you?

I wouldn't really say I have a set routine or a serious focus on scales, though I have made it a point to play the major scale and blues scale in all twelve positions. I've always found myself in situations where I've been forced to use my ears and improvise. I like to scan the radio and play along with whatever comes across the air. I also like to play chords on the piano and experiment with which notes work well over them.

What would you say is the most valuable thing that you've learned about music? And how did you learn it?

I learned early on about the role of each instrument in the band. Shortly after I started playing the harmonica, I started learning other instruments and began making backing tracks. Having this knowledge has been extremely helpful. Also, learning another instrument, especially a chordal instrument like guitar or piano, is a great way to become a better harmonica player. When you have an idea of what notes make up the chords, you have a clearer picture in your mind of what notes on the harmonica work best and why.

Do you play other instruments besides harmonica, and if so, which ones?

I play piano, organ, a little bit of bass, and a tiny bit of drums.

Your music is so pure and so soulful. How do you get the feeling across to the listener? And could you describe your feelings when you play?

When you really dig in and feel your music, your audience will usually feel it too. Excitement and emotion are contagious, and music in and of itself has a very spiritual element to begin with. I usually don't play a song that doesn't first move me in some way. In the same way that a singer puts their heart and soul into a song as they sing, I try to express the same thing through my instrument.

Your vibrato is beautiful. How would you best describe your technique?

I attribute my throat vibrato to my biggest harp hero and

influence, the late Terry McMillan. Early on, I spent hours and hours trying to emulate his sound until it became embedded deep into my spirit. Buddy Greene was another influence who has a great vibrato and such a smooth style. I listened to his music for hours on end. In those days, there was no YouTube or software to give you pointers—you had to rely on your ears. Sometimes the time you spend simply listening is just as important as time spent playing.

Which musicians have inspired you in the past, and what about them did you find inspiring?

I always go back to Terry McMillan, because I knew that was the sound I wanted. His tone was arguably the best ever, with such warm, round-sounding notes. I also appreciated his arrangements and approach to some of the classic hymns when he released his *I've Got a Feelin'* album around 1992. That album really helped me start thinking of new ways to arrange and breathe life into some of the old hymns and songs I'd grown up with. I also loved Charlie McCoy, and though I didn't have access to a lot of his music in the early days, the albums I did have really helped me master the country-style patterns and helped me develop my speed. Charlie was a true pioneer of advancing the harmonica beyond the limits of strictly blues playing.

Who currently inspires you, and why?

As far as harmonica players, I would say Howard Levy for his note selection and the way he makes the harmonica come alive over such nice chord progressions. He's so much more than just a great harmonica player, he's a musical genius. I also love to hear Carlos del Junco, Steve Baker, Pt Gazell, Pat Bergeson, and Mitch Kashmar. All have such great phrasing and style and are so refreshing to listen to. And I love listening to an amazing guitar player, Phil Keaggy, who's pretty well-known in the Christian music world. I've learned so much from studying his work.

How do you approach learning a new piece of music?

I play by ear as I always have, so if I hear a new song that I'm interested in learning, I'll spend a lot of time listening to it or singing along before I ever pick up the harmonica.

What is your approach to note selection and harmony?

My note selection is determined by the chord progressions. I like to find ways to play what I think sounds the best. On some of my recordings, I often play a harmony part, which may involve a different tuning or sometimes even a different harp in another position.

How important is music theory to you?

Very important. I have some basic knowledge of theory, but this is one area where I need to become more knowledgeable. This also comes in handy when sitting in with other musicians.

Do you have a favorite musical key?

I love the sound of the sharps and flats, but for me it all depends on the song and what kind of feeling or mood I'm trying to create. Key selection is also an important factor that many people tend to overlook. Every key tends to have its own mood and ability to evoke different emotions. I even believe that there are many songs that have become hit songs through the years, due in part to the key selection.

Do you have a favorite position?

I usually prefer second for both major and minor tunes, but I also like experimenting with ninth position and eleventh. Of course, it all depends on the tune. In recent years, I've fallen in love with third position major, which really opens up some awesome possibilities. For certain songs, it's simply the best choice. I also use third or fifth position for minor tunes if I'm after a specific type of sound or expression on certain notes.

What harmonica do you most regularly use, and why?

I mainly use Golden Melodies and have since very early on. I like the equal-temperament tuning since I do a lot of single-note melody playing, and I love the shape and feel of the Golden Melody in my hands. The full-length covers also seem to warm up the tone, especially on the higher keys.

Do you use any special tuning schemes? If so, could you describe the benefits?

For many years, I've been tuning the seven-draw note down a half step, which some in recent years have referred to as the "Todd Parrott tuning," though I was certainly not the first to use it. Players like Johnny Mars, J. J. Milteau, Nilo Guzman, and others have been known to use this tuning also. Pete Elder really deserves the credit for turning me on to the flat seven-draw tuning. This tuning gives you the flat third (B flat on a C harp) in second position without having to overblow hole six, but this is not why I use this tuning. The coolest thing about this tuning is that it allows you to bend the seven blow, which is extremely useful, not only in second position, but in other positions as well. Likewise, the seven-draw note is great to have in positions like eleventh, twelfth. Of course, you can overblow six, but sometimes it just doesn't sound as smooth or pretty. I'm all for using whatever works best for the song. Just because you can overblow doesn't mean it's always the best option.

What is your view on the lip-purse versus tongue-block debate?

It's really a non-issue to me, but I'm sure it's one of those things that will continue to be debated for years to come. There are certainly great players who tongue-block and lip-purse, and some that use both. I think part of the debate involves tone, but I think you can certainly have a great tone using either technique.

You are a player who uses overblows/overdraws. How important are those techniques to you?

Overblows and overdraws have become more important to me in recent years, especially since getting into custom harps, but I use them mostly for the needed expression in the higher octave of the harp. Being able to bend up the six overblow, as well as the seven overdraw, has become a very useful and soulful technique and sound for me. I find uses for all of the overblows and overdraws in many tunes and solos, and having custom harps from Joe Spiers has enabled me to accomplish things that were not possible in the past on stock harps. His work is amazing and eliminates all of the noises and squeals often associated with overblows and overdraws.

Do you get very nervous when performing? If so, how do you deal with it?

Sometimes I get nervous, but mainly when playing for other harp players, because they know when you make a mistake. However, whether playing for a harmonica-playing or non-harmonica-playing audience, I find that getting lost in and feeling the music is an easy cure for any nervousness.

When did you first start teaching the harmonica?

I've taught harmonica off and on since the early nineties. I started offering to teach via Skype simply because I love helping other harmonica players, and I think it's important to share what you've learned.

Do you teach students with varying levels of ability?

In the beginning, I tried to focus on players who were already intermediate players and were looking for new ideas or licks, or ways to incorporate overblows and overdraws into their playing. More recently, I've been doing much more work with beginners, including six-week courses and on Skype. It's really rewarding to watch a beginner progress and develop good habits and bends that are in tune. There also seems to be an interest lately in country licks and patterns, which I've been teaching for many years now.

What's the best bit of advice you could give to someone learning to play the harmonica?

My advice would be to learn another instrument, preferably a chordal instrument. It's also extremely helpful to work on your rhythm. As a teenager, I used to have a friend who loved to make up beats and rhythms, and I would play along on the harmonica, trying to play notes that matched his drum fills. I still do this. Many licks that I play are often based on drum fills or rhythms.

What has music done for you?

Music has brought a lot of happiness into my life and has allowed me to travel to some pretty neat places and make some really great friendships. Music has also allowed me to share a lot of joy with others through the years, which has been very rewarding. There are so many great people in the harmonica community.

Chapter 23

Annie Raines: Queen of the Blues

Photo courtesy of Joseph A. Rosen

Billboard has called Annie Raines "a rare female ace blues harmonica blower, as strong an acoustic country harp accompanist as she is a harder-edged, electrified Chicago-style lead player à la the great Little Walter." Perhaps Pinetop Perkins says it best about this queen of the blues harmonica: "She plays so good it hurts!"

Growing up in Newton, Massachusetts, Annie Raines took

piano lessons in grade school and later bought a synthesizer keyboard. Then she saw *The Buddy Holly Story* and switched to real instruments. In junior high school, she was also fascinated with juggling, and on her seventeenth birthday, decided to buy *Juggling for the Complete Klutz*. The bookstore didn't have it, so she settled for a similar title, Jon Gindick's *Country and Blues Harmonica for the Musically Hopeless*. Raines took up the harmonica and began going to a weekly Sunday blues jam, her church. A few months before her high school graduation, she made her stage debut at the 1369 Jazz Club in Cambridge.

Raines briefly attended Antioch College and then dropped out to pursue her musical career as one of America's few female blues harmonica players. She played the New England club circuit and traveled to Chicago to play with many of her musical idols, including Pinetop Perkins, James Cotton, and Louis Myers. While working on the regional blues circuit and teaching harmonica, she met and began working with blues guitarist Paul Rishell. They had an instant connection, started working together, and have been together since, now twenty-two years. Says Raines, "Paul and I have been musical partners for the last twenty-two years and a crazy married couple for the last seven or so. We're still trying to work our way backward to dating!"

Raines and Rishell tour together, collaborate on original songs, and have released award-nominated albums *Moving to the Country* (which won the W. C. Handy Award for Acoustic Blues Album), *Goin' Home*, and *A Night in Woodstock*, playing a wide range of blues styles from Blind Lemon Jefferson and Son House to Little Walter.

Raines plays harp, mandolin, piano, and sings. The twosome are featured in the music documentary *Chasin' Gus' Ghost*; have performed on *A Prairie Home Companion*, *Late Night with Conan O'Brien*, and PBS's *Arthur*; and have performed and recorded with Susan Tedeschi, John Sebastian, Pinetop Perkins, and Rory Block. Susan Tedeschi recorded an "unplugged" version of Paul's *Blues on a Holiday* with Paul and Annie for her 2003 release, *Wait for Me*.

What put you on your musical path? Was it the piano?

I think the piano helped a lot by giving me early musical training. I was drawn to music, but I wasn't a prodigy. I went to services every Saturday and sang in Hebrew, and while I didn't know the words, I liked the melodies, so I learned to fake my way and would sort of mumble in key. I feel that somehow led me to playing the harmonica.

So you read Jon Gindick's book and then taught yourself?

Yes. And then I started getting into Muddy Waters. Jerry Portnoy was one of the first harp players I'd ever heard. Muddy had already passed away, but I ended up taking a couple of lessons from Jerry, who was a huge influence on me through his music. I was also a member of the Cambridge Harmonica Orchestra, and all these great players were all into the old stuff. There were a lot of people really hungry to be better players.

What was the Cambridge Harmonica Orchestra (CHO)?

The CHO was started in the late seventies to fill in the bill for a local arts festival in Cambridge, started by Otis Reed and Pierre Beauregard, who was both the musical director and inventor of alternate-tuned harmonicas. Pierre wrote arrangements for groups of harmonica players to play rock 'n' roll, R&B, and blues. It was a really high-energy band. I was recruited by one of the keyboard players and had to audition for Pierre. Pierre said, "Can you bend a note?" I think I was like, "Yeah, I can." So he gave me a CHO T-shirt—that was my audition. I got to play in the rhythm section. I didn't get to take a solo for three years, but I got a really good workout, learning parts and huffing and puffing and chugging.

And you also play mandolin?

In 1998, Paul handed me a mandolin that belonged to his late wife and said, "I need you to play these parts on songs that I'm writing." So I learned a few chords, and he taught me a few chords, and then I learned a few more chords. The mandolin is pretty compatible with the harmonica because the strings are tuned a fifth apart.

What are your favorite kinds of blues to play?

My first love is Chicago blues—that still takes me back. I feel totally involved, and I don't only mean Jimmie Rodgers–style early-fifties Chicago blues. Little Walter–style sound had a lot of atmosphere and space.

Do you have any favorite songs?

Just about anything on Jimmy Rogers' *Chicago Bound*, my go-to album. If I could have only one album, that would be it. My favorite harmonica songs are "A Little Bit Closer" and Muddy Waters' "Just to Be with You"; Jerry McCain's "Steady" is one of my all-time favorites.

Who do you listen to for inspiration?

I still go back to Little Walter for inspiration, as well as Jimmy Rogers and Sonny Boy Williamson II, also known as Rice Miller.

Do you think that scales practice is important?

I think a little bit can go a long way depending on what you are trying to do. Your muscle memory is the primary mechanical push in learning to play, so by playing the scales and getting the transitions between notes under your fingertips or under your lips, you will be getting acquainted with the instrument in different ways.

Do you practice scales anymore, or do you have enough muscle memory that you don't have to?

I occasionally force myself to practice them, but I hate practicing. So the way I try to improve is mostly by playing and by keeping a sense of play about it. I learn much more from playing on stage than from playing alone.

Do you practice at all, or are you out there playing all the time?

I'm not out there playing as much as I would like, and I don't practice the harmonica as much as I used to, but I practice all the instruments. I'm a student of tap-dance and I try to sing and I practice the mandolin and I'm learning guitar, and I practice chromatic to try to align myself with where the notes are.

You also teach?

I started teaching when I was around nineteen and have been giving classes and private lessons for twenty-five years. I have the occasional Skype students and I made a video for TrueFire a couple of years ago called *Blues Harmonica Blueprint*. I tried to download what I'd taught up to that point, because I really wanted to explain myself in my debut. I didn't want to make a partial representation of what I wanted to do. The company wanted me to make a video for beginners, and I wanted to make one with an intermediate style of playing. It ended up being four hours long with thirty-five pages of tab! (You can purchase it at www.paulandannie.com.)

Do you find that there is a big difference between teaching by Skype as opposed to in person?

The big difference is you can't play together in real time because of the slight delay, but it is possible to have rapport on the screen. And it is so much easier to communicate through the visual medium of Skype than on the telephone. There is some degree of musical give-and-take in real time.

Do you teach everyone the same, or do you teach each person differently?

I teach each person totally differently, which is why it was so difficult to make a video. Every person varies so much in terms of learning styles and their musical abilities or lack of abilities. I have been lucky to have some lovely students. It is just really fun to learn from them, too.

What would be the best piece of advice you would give to someone learning to play the harmonica?

Almost everybody, no matter on what level they are, needs to learn more about rhythm. Whether a person is a beginner or an advanced player, I might show them a shuffle pattern. Some more advanced players already know shuffle patterns, so I will start teaching them about the underpinnings of the music, the structure of it, the rhythm, the bass lines, and the accents—things like that.

Little Walter is constantly playing rhythm, in-and-out rhythm chords between his licks, so if you just learn the licks, you are not really learning the song; you are not really learning how to breathe and how to move. As a tap student, too, I'm getting deeply involved in the tap of things and the movement and the fact that certain motions are executed in time. Now I think of playing as really dancing on the harmonica.

Can you tap and play at the same time?

Not yet. I'm just doing one or the other; my tap-dancing has a long way to go.

And are you tap-dancing in shows?

Paul and I are working on something together; we're actually doing it at shows, but still under the radar. He plays solo guitar and I tap-dance to it like the old street musicians did. It's given me a lot of insight into the roots of early blues and jazz.

How do you learn a new song? By ear?

Memorizing things never comes easily to me. I just go to the part that I like, then I will remember what's to either side of it, and then, after hearing it incidentally around three hundred thousand times, I will probably know most of it and will go ahead and fine-tune it. Right now, I'm learning keyboard parts to sixties pop and rock songs for a band we're putting together. It's kind of a layered process; it takes a lot of time for stuff to come together, but I'll work on it, listen to it actively, sing along, listen to it without playing, listen to it passively while I'm doing something else—I just need to try and reach all the different corners of my brain.

Have you ever had a period when you were uninspired, feeling that you were playing the same riffs?

Definitely. Paul's first wife, Leslie, was our manager and really knew how to make things run. She died in 1996 of breast cancer after two years with it. Not only was her death devastating on a personal level, it left us essentially rudderless. We basically had not built up that much of a career at that point. I ended up taking on a lot of the booking and tried to be a good booking agent and a good manager, and I felt like I was terrible at it. But I learned a lot of things while trying to hustle gigs and learn how to negotiate and how to manage things on the road; I think I really didn't devote a lot of time to developing musically for about a ten-year period. I was learning how to sing and play mandolin, and I progressed a little bit, but I really felt that for many years, I was repeating myself. I think I'm working my way off that spot, but I really was in shock for a long time.

How do you make an intermediate player better? What is the best piece of advice you can give them?

I would tell an intermediate player keep doing what you are doing, keep studying that material, keep studying and learning. Work on rhythm and tone and keeping time with your whole body. I also have acquired a few tricks over the years, and one of them is if you listen to certain Big Walter recordings over and over again, your tone is going to get better; you'll have a better tone if you just listen. Listening is a big part of playing. If that sound is in your ears, it will be natural for you to want to express it.

What advice do you have for advanced players? What's the most important thing for them to learn?

Advanced players should play with other people as much as they can, and that is advice for everybody. Go to jams and get your stage time. You can only learn more as an improviser. When you play with other musicians, you also learn stage etiquette, which means finding your spots, leaving space, and not stepping on people's toes. This makes you more musical.

What is being musical?

Being musical is about making the listener more musical, so instead of playing some notes, you let the person listening hear the note in their head—then you are really communicating with them.

What has music done for you?

I think music has kept me alive. It has ruined me; it has taught me to live with contradiction. It has taught me a lot of values that I really want to apply in my life, such as leaving space and letting things flow, not trying to control them too much, and not thinking too much. Thinking is the enemy of music.

Chapter 24

Jason Ricci: Standing Shoulder to Shoulder with the Greats

Photo courtesy of Kris Ciesliga

Blues Music Award winner Jason Ricci is a **passionate**, self-made harp master, New Orleans Saints fan, cat lover, former drug addict, and former convict. He has overcome every obstacle, including bipolar disorder, to take to the road again with a new band, better than ever. "When they update the history of blues harmonica fifty years from now, Jason Ricci will have a place of honor, much as Walter and Butterfield do now," says Adam Gussow. "He's one of a handful of contemporary blues harmonica players who can stand shoulder to shoulder with the greats of the past, including Little Walter—he's that good, that creative, that original, that revolutionary, and that influential. Together with Sugar Blue and Carlos del Junco, he defines the modern sound, but he's also a master of traditional approaches."

"The musicianship that he has and the knowledge he has of that instrument and music in general is mind-boggling," says Nick Moss. "He's not just a guy who knows his instrument and is a technical genius, but he's a showman of the best kind because he has all the tools to back up his showmanship." Winslow Yerxa says, "He is incredibly encouraging of others and very articulate in helping other people, and that is rare. For someone of his caliber as a player and his level of achievement to be able to turn from being a performer to a teacher is something I find remarkable."

Brought up in Portland, Maine, Ricci sang in a punk band with a friend and started playing harmonica. Says Ricci, "I think the band chose it for me because I couldn't really ruin them like if I had a bass or a guitar, which can really damage the music, but the harmonica could only make it worse a little bit."

Your mother told you to take harmonica lessons; how did that happen?

She said that she would buy me a harmonica, but I had to take lessons because she didn't know they were so cheap. We all thought that they were going to be a lot of money—that's the only reason I agreed to take any lessons, because otherwise, I never would've met the guy who really taught me how to play music.

Pat Ramsey?

Pat Ramsey was my main influence in harmonica, but he wasn't actually my harmonica teacher. He was the reason I moved to Memphis when I was twenty-one. I was driving home from college and stopped in Memphis and heard him. That was the best harmonica I'd ever heard, so I decided to move there and go see him once a week in Tunica and two nights a week in Memphis. Nowadays kids have YouTube videos and everybody's accessible, but back in those days, if you wanted to hear somebody play, you had to move to where they lived.

Can you talk about your drug use?

I was doing drugs when I was eighteen, but by the time I was twenty-four living in Mississippi, my drugs and alcohol use got bad. I moved to Florida in 1998 and cleaned up and was clean for eleven and one-half years after that. Then the band broke up, my house got flooded, and my bipolar disorder was running pretty rampant. My boyfriend of five years left me. It was more than I could handle. I wasn't really that happy. I had gotten everything I wanted out of life—all materialistic things, like a house and a car and a cool band and a record label and booking agents and tour dates. That's what I wanted, and when I got all that stuff, I wasn't happy because that stuff is not important in the long run.

I was really miserable, so I got high because that's what addicts and alcoholics do. I had just spent my whole life trying to replace drugs and alcohol with those things, and I did a really good job. A lot of addicts and alcoholics have such an incredible drive to fill that void with something, but there's never enough alcohol or drugs. I was without a spiritual solution.

How did you quit?

I went to a treatment center in Florida for ninety days, and then left and got high again and committed some crimes to get more money for dope. I didn't get caught. I just turned myself in to the police because I wanted to get sober and the treatment center would not take me back. The judge was pretty cool and gave me a year and a day at another treatment center. For nine months, I was locked up, and then they put me in a work-release situation. I spent three years on probation in Florida for that.

What about being bipolar?

There are a lot of people out there who are bipolar and afraid to take medication. It's really difficult for musicians when you take medication because your creative process is completely turned upside down and doesn't make any sense anymore. I think it's important that people make choices to live and not just make silly decisions about "Oh well, I'd rather die and write a song" now. I have been off of bipolar meds and it's not by choice, it's because my body can no longer handle them.

How long were you with Jason Ricci and New Blood?

Eleven years, touring three hundred days a year.

What was life like on the road being the front man?

It was fun for the first three or four years, and then after that it was a lot of work.

What was it like being in an alpha-male world of musicians when you had a different gender preference, and have you changed preferences?

I'm married to a woman now. I didn't really change preferences; I've always liked men and women. I just can't help it; I'm attracted to both genders.

Johnny Winter called you in 2012 and said he wanted you on his record.

It was incredible. It's pretty hard to come up with words to describe what it's like when somebody you've admired your whole life wants you on his record—it's humbling, surreal, bizarre, flattering.

Jason Ricci: Standing Shoulder to Shoulder with the Greats

You're a master harp player and a world-class musician. How do beginners master that technique?

The most important thing people starting out can learn is just to be a really good listener. I know a lot of musicians who have natural talent but haven't developed an ability to just listen. What's the song saying? What's the vibe? What does it feel like, what does it do to you? Put the harmonica down for a second. When I used to take lessons from guys like my first harmonica teacher, David Daniels, and this other guy in Maine named D. W. Gill, I would frequently show up at their house, and I didn't play one week. I just sat there with a tape recorder. I might ask a question or two, or I might play for a second and say, "Hey listen, when I'm doing this, this is what happens," and then for an hour they'd talk and I'd just record the lesson and listen and let them share their experience. But people are impatient and want things right away.

Have you ever had a period when you were uninspired?

I'm very interested in melody and rhythm and harmony, which are the basic building blocks of music. If you're interested in those subjects, you learn pretty quickly that there's an infinite amount of shit that you can do. I've had tremendously long periods of uninspiration, where I just didn't care about playing any of it. Sure, I've had uninspired years.

Did you put down the instrument or play through it?

Before I moved to New Orleans, I put it down for six months. I was also way more interested in smoking crack than playing harmonica. You better be sure you really love something if you make it your job, because part of that love is going to change. It will never be the same as when it was new and wonderful and holy. They say the Latin root of the word *amateur* is "for the love of it," and that *professional* means money—you get paid to do it. When it's your profession, even when you don't want to do it, you still fucking have to.

What did you learn from Pat Ramsey?

Everything; a lot about my phrasing, to think differently about harmonica. Just look at the way it sits on top of music, the way you can navigate, chord changes. Everything doesn't have to be the way I've heard it. He opened the door for me. Harmonica is more like a lead guitar instead of like the way Little Walter was doing it, which is incredible, but Pat Ramsey was like Butterfield on steroids. Pat changed everything for me. There is no Jason Ricci without a Pat Ramsey.

What do you do differently from him?

The primary difference has to do with timing. Also, I had a humongous Little Walter influence prior to meeting Pat. I retained a lot of that, because I have a love and affinity for traditional blues harmonica, in particular Little Walter, but also George Smith and James Cotton and Junior Wells. Pat didn't have a real infatuation with Little Walter.

I wanted to learn the overblow so that I could play chromatically, and Pat was never really interested in that. A lot of my style has to do with having a traditional blues influence. I'm really interested in New Orleans street beats and pushing and pulling elements of swing. And I'm really interested melodically in chromatic melodies, jazz-type melodies, and being able to appreciate some of the chords that come at me that are not one-four-fives.

How do scales inspire your playing?

Scales are a lot of fun because I don't have to think about the notes that are in a chord. It's the opposite of harmony. I have a scale that I can use as a five-note treatment of any given chord progression. Only having those five notes, it doesn't mean that I don't think harmonically, because I do.

How do these five notes apply to these three chords? That's, of course, ever-changing, as the chords change, but it's simplified. I always tell my students, the less you have to think about what note you're going to play next, the more time you have to think about how you're going to play that note. If you only have five notes that you're focusing on, that forces you to think of time more. It also forces you to think about tone more.

As far as time is concerned, I'm saying I have more time to actually think about time and how those five notes actually could swing or not. If I'm only thinking about just those five notes, say, in a pentatonic scale, my cat brain can process better and I can start working on placing those notes in places around the snare and kick that will make the music move.

So, I have all this extra time because I'm only focusing on five notes. It's like self-imposed prison, where you learn to gain appreciation for a small group of notes that can compose various melodies, and the other areas of your music improve tremendously.

Do you tongue-block or lip-purse or both?

Both. It depends on the type of music. If I'm looking for something really rhythmic, I'm actually going to tongue-block. If I'm playing a regular shuffle in second or third position or first position, and it's like a regular blues, like a Jimmy Reed–type thing, I'm going to tongue-block, because I'm a big fan of the way that sounds. But if I'm playing something that's jazzy and I want lots of staccato or want the ability to move around really, really fast and really, really butter, and I don't want clunky, rhythm types of choral influence coming in between each note, I'm not going to tongue-block, because the temptation to play it that way is great. A lot of people say, "Oh, you get better tone tongue-blocking." I don't agree with that.

What's your favorite kind of music?

I don't have one. When I get into the bathtub, all I want to hear is fifties bebop or classical music. The past six months, it's just been Chopin; it's really all I want to hear—just the piano pieces are all I'm interested in.

Who do you suggest students listen to in order to improve their playing?

You can't do any better than Little Walter if you're interested in blues harmonica. He covered so many basics. I would love to get into a big debate with people who believe that Little Walter didn't really think much about music or that he wasn't familiar with certain ideas on an academic level, because I think he was. He was magic.

You've been teaching lessons on Skype?

Yes. You can find me at www.mooncat.org. Anybody who wants to take a Skype lesson should email me.

How do you make an intermediate player better?

For me, the intermediate player is somebody who can listen to music on his own and figure it out and then regurgitate it back in a similar manner. I would say the formal study of melody, rhythm, and harmony with any kind of teacher, even if it's a bass player or a piano player, is what's going to give somebody the tools to never, ever have to listen to music ever again to get ideas.

All things are music. All things are vibrations. If you get into studying music, what you discover is that it's nothing but numbers in mathematics. Of course there are cracks—there are spaces between one and one and a half, spaces between one and one and a quarter—that's where the magic is, but we can learn what the system is and how it's laid out. Surround yourself with other pros. Then, if you want to go from intermediate to advanced, you've got to be around advanced musicians.

Anything else you want the harmonica world to know?

Year after year, the harmonica world has been incredible to me. I'm so lucky and so thankful for people like Adam Gussow and

Winslow Yerxa—without Winslow, I don't know what I would have done all these years. And the blues community at large. The Blues Foundation paid for me to go to rehab, and for me to win that award from the Blues Foundation was incredible. As a way of life, playing harmonica for a living is hard, frequently no fun, and spiritually, financially, intellectually, and emotionally challenging. But thank you to the blues and the harmonica community for giving me the opportunity to do this.

What has music done for you?

It's ruined my life, and it's given me something to live for.

Chapter 25

Wade Schuman: The Pied Piper of Hazmat Modine

Photo courtesy of Dave Clough Photography

"Hazmat Modine" sounds like a dangerous heated chemical, because hazmat means hazardous material and Modine is a company that manufactures heating products; but no, Hazmat Modine is not dangerous, just a dangerously talented eight-piece band including diatonic harmonica, tuba, saxophone, clarinet, accordion, banjo, guitar, and drums. Bandleader and front man Wade Schuman is a multi-instrumentalist (harmonica, zamponia (pan flute), and lute-guitar), lead vocalist, songwriter, producer, and album designer.

"Hazmat Modine was Wade Schuman's concept, and to see it come from nothing to an international group is amazing," says Joe Filisko. "Wade is unique because he's a man who wears more hats than I could possibly name: he's an amazing harmonica player, singer, front man, bandleader, and visionary. When you look at the first Hazmat Modine CD with its photos, layout, and design, you're really looking at Wade's soul and how deep and creative a person he can be."

Schuman, who founded the band in the late 1990s, produced the band's first album, *Hazmat Modine – Bahamut* (Jaro Medien/ Barbes Records), in 2006. He wrote most of the music, sang vocals, and played diatonic harp and other instruments. The album, which took seven years to produce, rose to number twelve on *Billboard's* Top Blues Albums chart. Reviewers called the sound primeval, authentically indigenous, otherworldly, and unlike any other music. Five years later, the band recorded its second album, *Cicada* (Jaro Medien/Barbes Records), and it was awarded Best 2011 Blues Album by the prestigious French Charles Cros Academy. Schuman produced an album, *Extra Deluxe Supreme*, which came out along with a live CD, and the band has released a new CD, *Box of Breath*.

Wade Schuman is a self-taught musician, and before forming the band, had never sung in public. He did, however, inherit his sociologist father's curiosity (and is passionate about zoology and natural sciences), and his mother, great-grandfather, and great-aunt's art genes. Schuman, who graduated from the Pennsylvania Academy of the Fine Arts, is not only a respected painter but is also full-time faculty and chair of faculty and the painting department at the New York Academy of Art.

As a child, Schuman loved to draw and planned to become an artist, but was also greatly influenced by his older brother, a musician who played piano, accordion, violin, and mandolin. Wade Schuman listened to his brother's pre-war blues, boogie-woogie, ragtime, Bulgarian, and Romanian music, as well as the Beatles, and contemporary rock of the early sixties and seventies. "I think the music that informs you the most is the music you hear when you're young," he says. "Certain things are embedded in you."

At the age of ten, Schuman took up harmonica because the instrument was easy to get. His first harmonica was a Lancer, a less-expensive diatonic Hohner made in Ireland. His brother bought him a record, *Harmonica Blues: Great Performances of the 1920s and '30s*, a collection of pre-war diatonic blues harmonica, and Schuman set out to learn it all. "There was no information, no internet, you just learned on your own," he says.

After high school graduation, Schuman attended the Rhode Island School of Design, but dropped out to hitchhike in Europe, Greece, Turkey, and Morocco, supporting himself by doing odd jobs and playing street harmonica. Upon his return, he studied painting at the Pennsylvania Academy of the Fine Arts. Around that time, he stopped playing harmonica because he thought the quality of harmonicas had gotten bad in the eighties and he was frustrated. His passion for the instrument was reignited by a new Suzuki harmonica and Steve Baker's *The Harp Handbook*.

Around that time, his wife encouraged him to enter a Philadelphia harmonica contest, and he played a fox chase he'd learned as a kid. "Nobody had heard of me because I wasn't a professional player, and nobody was expecting this weird guy to play," says Schuman. "Everyone expected Steve Guyger to win." (The first prize was split between Guyger and Schuman.)

When Kim Field's book on the history of harmonica was published, Schuman cold-called him and the two became friends. The same happened with Joe Filisko, who at the time "had been hooked up with Madcat and wasn't playing pre-war stuff. I was the only person I knew who could play that style. Now, of course, Joe is the best there is," Schuman says.

At the time, Schuman was making his living teaching art and painting commissions, though he played harp in a small bar band on Friday nights. "I didn't sing, and I wasn't the bandleader," he says. "I just played, but I was really influenced by Kim and Joe and Steve Guyger." In the early nineties, Schuman met Pat Missin and began experimenting with alternate tunings using the pre-war techniques he knew. "But I still wasn't really a professional," says Schuman. Then he recorded harmonica on a few songs on Joan Osborne's first album.

In 1997, Schuman moved to New York and met Rob Paparozzi, and they started a professional harmonica get-together group, "The New York Reedsters." Members included Pierre Beauregard, Howard Levy, Joe Filisko, Pat Missin, Charlie Leighton, Chamber Huang, Robert Bonfiglio, and Adam Gussow. The group met a couple of times a year at Wade Schuman's NYC midtown loft. "It was a room full of the most curious egos in the world, because you had the early vaudeville harmonica guys, including the Sgro Brothers, from Elmira, New York, classical guys like Huang and Bonfiglio, blues guys, and Levy guys," says Schuman.

At the meet-up, Schuman discovered that Randy Weinstein, a chromatic and diatonic harmonica player, shared his same interests. The two decided to form a band. "My original idea was to have four harmonica players," says Schuman, "but I could never find any other harmonica players that would have either a diverse-enough skill base or diverse set of musical interests. Chromatic guys basically play jazz or classical. The diatonic guys basically play blues or jazz, but none of them play a lot of the music in which I was interested." Schuman tried to convert Dennis Gruenling to the band, but Gruenling, then, mainly was playing West Coast jump blues.

Schuman wanted a tuba, at least two harmonicas, and a guitar. "At first, I didn't know who was going to do vocals, because I had never sung in public," he says, "but I became the main singer. We got a woman who played percussion and was classically trained, so it was a guitar, two harmonicas, tuba, and drums—five musicians, the beginning of Hazmat Modine."

Wade Schuman: The Pied Piper of Hazmat Modine

"Wade wanted a big band," says Erik Della Penna, who has known Schuman since 1994, and for the last two years has been Hazmat Modine's guitar/banjo/songwriter. "And naiveté carries you through," says Della Penna. "Wade made it happen with the force of his talent, vision, and relentless personality. He's an artist first—this band is just a canvas for him. He's got a quirky personality; probably his greatest strength is he can make things happen just by his exuberance and enthusiasm."

In 1998, Hazmat Modine played at Schuman's best friend's wedding. A guest approached Schuman and said, "Oh, you're good. You should play at my friend's club." The club, Terra Blues in NYC's Greenwich Village, booked the band. "It was the very first gig I booked," says Schuman, "but neither the guitar player nor the tuba player could make it, and that was half the band. The new tuba player was Joe Daley, who had toured the world with Taj Mahal and played the Fillmore East with Jefferson Airplane." Daley continues to play with Hazmat Modine. Says Schuman, "At that time, I was primarily a painter, not a professional musician. But Joe heard something in me and completely supported me. In a sense, he raised me as a bandleader and a musician. I wouldn't be who I am if it weren't for Joe."

Joe Daley is equally effusive. "Most harmonica players use the instrument to fill in spaces," Daley says. "They'll sing, do the harmonica thing—Wade's harmonica playing is phenomenal, and the harmonica is a major player on the stage. He becomes the Pied Piper and brings the band along with him."

It's hard to define Hazmat Modine's music, which fuses styles from blues and jazz to calypso and NOLA. It is not traditional music, although the band evolved at the time there was resurgence in roots-based New York music. Says Schuman, "American music is informed by the immigrant experience. In essence, American music is world music, since it is a product of the all diasporas that have come here."

Schuman feels that to be faithful to the music forms that made American music great, you have to be faithful to what made it great, not to the music forms themselves. "American music is, by its essence, music that comes out of the so-called melting pot of different cultures banging up against each other," he says.

Schuman calls himself a folk musician whose approach is to follow his intuition. "I've also been lucky to have good musicians around me, and I'm greedy. I really love trumpets. When I first had the trumpet, it was no, we don't want another musician, there's too many. We already had five people. Then I wanted saxophone, but why would we have six people, it's too much. And then we got a trombone player—we don't need a trombone player, we already have enough people in the band. Why do we need two guitars? We already have one guitarist. But I knew how I wanted to do this, and I made it work somehow. Most bands fall apart. It's a huge job—I mean, to have nine people in the band, it's ridiculous."

As Schuman worked on the first album for seven years, musicians came and went. He'd heard throat singers from the Russian Republic of Tuva perform. "Tuvan music is one of the most musical cultures in the world," says Schuman. "These guys were like the Beatles of Tuva; they did a sold-out show at the Symphony Space, came over the next morning, and we played together in my studio. It was like magic. We recorded two songs, and they're on *Bahamut*."

Schuman also connected with Gangbé, an African band from Benin and which Schuman thought was "the coolest band in the world." Schuman pursued Gangbé, but the two bands were always on different continents. Four years later, they finally connected and recorded together in Europe. Says Schuman, "If I have an idea, I'm going to see it through, even if takes me forever. That's how I do things—I just try."

Schuman says that what makes the band original is that the songs are idiosyncratic to the band. "You have to create and move ahead, especially with a band that's almost twenty years old. In the new album, the songs are much more about stories and lyrics, more melodic, less about solos and virtuosity."

Schuman is no longer that involved with the harmonica world.

His focus is more on being a songwriter, front man, and producer. He also isn't really interested in long solos. "When I listen to all the old blues guys, they kind of play the same song," he says. "They didn't do lots of solos—that's a very modern thing. The problem I have with most contemporary harmonica playing is they're playing to impress each other; they're playing endless solos to show other harmonica players how good they are. Nobody really cares that much outside of the harmonica world. The average person wants to relate to a musician, to the singer, to the melody— they don't want endless soloing. That's one of the problems in the harmonica world; it can at times be so very insular."

Schuman, who at one time had an endorsement with Seydel, is now endorsed by Hohner. "Both make a great product," he says. "I've gotten a lot of support from the harmonica world, but I only have so much time; the truth is, for an eight-piece band, there is not so much money touring in the harmonica world. Or blues world to support a band this size. We generally play jazz festivals and world music festivals, and sometimes, rock festivals. I would love to do more blues festivals, I'd love to do New Orleans, but it's very hard to make a living that way."

Schuman's harmonica heroes include Deford Bailey, Paul Butterfield, Gwen Foster, Jaybird Coleman, Joe Filisko, Howlin' Wolf, Peg Leg Sam, and Charles Leighton. He is also fond of Son of Dave, who was with an indie band in the nineties and has reinvented himself as a one-man band. "He's a great harmonica player," Schuman says, "but it's not about chops. It's really about the music. He just layers these sounds and he writes songs and he is a great singer." Hazmat Modine has a collaboration with Son of Dave on the new CD on a song called "Lazy Time."

Schuman's goal is to seduce the audience, "not only to make them feel good, but to *move* them," he says. And judging from the audience's reactions and demands for encores—everywhere from NYC's Terra Blues to Europe and beyond—that is exactly what Wade Schuman and his band are doing, mesmerizing the audience as he plays to them, the Pied Piper of Hazmat Modine.

Chapter 26

Indiara Sfair: Harmonica Goddess

Photo courtesy of Fernando Hideki

Brazilian harmonica player Indiara Sfair plays with such love and joy it's no wonder she has been called a harmonica goddess. Her fans on YouTube say her playing gives them goose pimples, that they've never heard playing like this before. Many say they wish it were two or three hours long instead of two minutes, and some say her playing says so much without talking.

Born and raised in Curitiba, Brazil, Sfair's parents had eclectic musical taste, and she was brought up listening to blues, rock 'n' roll, New Age, and Brazilian. Her first instrument was a children's piano.

At the age of fifteen, she was given a harmonica as a birthday present, and soon after, she was playing in a band. In 2011 she recorded an EP for a band with whom she played, Tic Tac Joe. She will soon be recording her own CD.

How old were you when you were exposed to music, and what kind of music?

Since I was conceived (hahaha), my parents always listened to music; my father even sang the blues. They were always into all kinds of music, especially classical music, blues, New Age, and Brazilian pop.

How old were you when you first heard live music? And what kind?

I was probably a few months old. My father sang in a few bands, and my mom always took us to shows and festivals. My stepfather was a great guitar player, my brother is a drummer, and my mother always encouraged us musically and artistically.

When did you take up harmonica? How old were you, and how did it happen?

A friend gave me my first harmonica for my fifteenth birthday. He knew I liked blues and musical instruments, so he chose harmonica. He had no idea that he was giving me something far more valuable than a harmonica.

Did you take lessons, or are you self-taught?

I tried to learn some melodies by ear and teach myself, but I didn't understand that there are several keys of the harmonica, so I couldn't do much. Years later, I learned from a harmonica player from my hometown, Benê Chireia. I also took classes with several different harmonica players, each of whom had a different style and way of teaching. I have always found it worthwhile to learn from several people.

Do you play any other instruments?

My main instrument is the harmonica, but I play a bit of piano, the guitar, flute, and tamborim.

Who were your favorite musicians, both non-harmonica players and harmonica players?

I would certainly say Eric Clapton and David Gilmour. I know that they are not harp players, but they were always the artists I admired the most. I am crazy about their songs! But, speaking about harp players, my favorite is Carlos del Junco. I love the melodies of his songs.

When did you start playing in a band?

It was about six months after I started learning playing harmonica. I didn't play very well at all, but in 2009 I got together with a great friend, Ricardo Maranhão, and we formed a blues duo called Double Blues. Now, we are about to release our first album!

In 2017, you went to Nashville and played in jam sessions at the blues club. What was that like?

As the blues is a musical style that has always been a part of American culture, I found the audience very receptive with the performances. I had the chance to be on stage with really great and generous musicians, and I learned a lot with some harp players from Nashville, specially Tim Gonzales—he is the best! I was amazed how great the musicians are in the US!

What was the Milk'n Blues Band, and how did it start?

We were friends, three boys and three girls, just having fun. We created blues versions of pop music and posted videos on the internet. The videos started to go viral, and there was a demand for shows. The next thing we knew, we were playing up to four shows a week, which turned into five years of me playing in this band. I miss them.

Why are there so few women harp players?

I think it's a cultural thing. Since instruments were created, they have been played mostly by men. It was the norm back then. But times are changing, and more women are now taking on more "masculine" roles.

What kind of harps did you start out with, and what do you play now?

I started with a very good diatonic harmonica of a Brazilian brand called Hering. Its cost-benefit was incredible, very cheap, and the sound was really good, but after I first tried a Hohner Marine Band 1896, I never wanted to play another harmonica. This harmonica fits me perfectly. It has a clean, bright sound, and in my opinion, it's the easiest to play. Anytime someone who's starting to play harp asks me what kind to play, I always recommend it.

Are they customized?

Not so far, but I plan to start using custom harmonicas.

What kind of mic do you play?

The sound with which I identify the most is the Shure SM58.

Do you use any effects?

I like to play with clean sound; the only effect I like to use is a little reverb.

What do you listen to for inspiration?

Everything, really.

Do you practice scales?

Not really, but I should. I put on backing tracks and play along with what I want to study.

What's your daily harmonica practice regimen, or is there one?

I don't have one. Sometimes I have many weeks without studying a single note.

Have you ever had a period when you were uninspired, and you felt as though you were playing the same riffs every time?

Absolutely! I always feel that.

How often do you tour, and where?

Each year, I'm traveling more with the opportunities that are coming my way. This year alone, I've had the opportunity to play at a festival in Canada, in Korea, and in many cities in Brazil.

What was it like playing with Buddy Guy?

I would say it was the best musical moment of my life to have the opportunity to share the stage with an idol, Mr. Buddy Guy. I will never forget it, and he was so generous! I was nervous, but my excitement was even greater.

Are there differences between US audiences and audiences of other countries? Do you play in a certain style depending on where you are?

Overall, in any country, it depends a lot on where you are performing. If it's a place where people go because of the music, generally the receptivity is very good; but if you're playing in a bar, where people go to eat, and the music is in the background, sometimes the audience is kind of cold. But, as the blues is a musical style that has always been a part of American culture ever since, the audience is very receptive and generous with the performances.

You've recorded a CD with two bands that you used to play with: one in 2015, and one in 2016. What kind of music was that?

Original songs; blues and folk music.

You are writing songs for your own CD. When do you think you'll be recording that?

My instrumental CD, hopefully, I will release at the end of this year. Next month, Ricardo Maranhão and I are releasing our first album together.

You are working on a harmonica method for beginners that will be available on your YouTube Channel. Is that www.youtube.com/user/indiharp?

Yes, it will be available on my YouTube Channel, www.youtube.com/c/IndiaraSfair.

What's the most important advice you give beginners?

Rather than play a lot once a week, play a little every day.

And for intermediates?

Finding your own way of playing. Play something that is true for you in some way. For me, the beautiful thing about music is to touch people in some way, and you do that by playing what is true for you.

What does the harmonica mean to you?

The harmonica, besides having a musical meaning, represents, in my life, the realization of everything I have always dreamed of.

It has shown me that with dedication, love, and work, we can reach our goals and be recognized for it. The harmonica brought me my greatest achievements, brought me many friends, and gave me a career. And this little instrument can really cry and express the feelings in a very true and unique way. It might be a very small instrument, but it is a very rich instrument. The harmonica has brought me my greatest achievements and has given me a wonderful career.

What does music mean for you?

Connection with the universe, with God. Music helps me to know myself; music is everything to me.

Chapter 27

Ronnie Shellist: Global Blues Harp Summit Ambassador

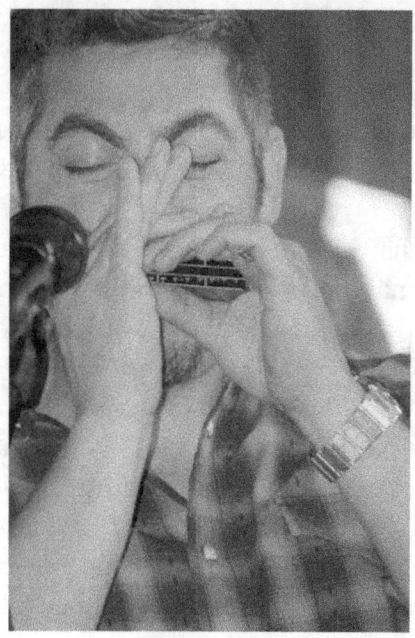

Photo courtesy of Jr. Wolfe

Noted blues harp player and harmonica teacher Ronnie Shellist has four rules for playing music: "Be passionate while you play, be free, know your instrument intimately, and relax—it's just music!" Born in Skokie, Illinois, and raised in Chicago until he was five years old, he then moved to Dallas, where he grew up.

Shellist's first real exposure to music was as a young teenager when his father purchased a small, inexpensive digital piano/organ and young Shellist would often play tunes with him.

When Shellist was fourteen, he picked up the guitar and took a few lessons, but didn't stay with that instrument for long. When he was twenty, his father bought himself a cheap harmonica and instruction booklet, and after his father had enough and put it down, Shellist decided he wanted to try it, too. By then, he was living in Austin, Texas, listening to as much live blues as he could. This hooked him on the blues harp.

Shellist began his musical career in 1997 working with Austin singer/songwriter Hugh Fadal. Blues great Gary Primich, living in Austin at the time, was also a huge influence on his music, as were Guy Forsyth and Walter T. Higgs. "If it weren't for those guys, I never would have pushed as hard as I did to learn how to get that sound out of my harp," says Shellist. In 1998, Shellist moved to Colorado and teamed up with the band Available Jones and toured the country with them.

In 2006, Shellist began posting performances on YouTube, which currently have over 10.5 million views. In the past fifteen years, he has worked with great Colorado locals John Alex Mason, Lionel Young, Rich Reno, Bob Pellegrino, and Erica Brown. He has opened live for B.B. King, Charlie Musselwhite, Robert Cray, and the Neville Brothers. His style, a combination of mostly Chicago and West Coast blues, is also influenced by funk and jazz. In 2007, Shellist recorded his first CD, *Chicago Sessions*, about which *Blues Revue* said: "The show belongs to Shellist's toneful harp." His CD *Till Then* has been called "chock full of superb blues harp, a nirvana for blues harp aficionados," Kim Wilson says. "Ronnie has a style on the harmonica all his own." Charlie Musselwhite calls Shellist "one fine player, and I ain't lyin'."

These days, Shellist is focused on offering online harmonica webinars called the Global Blues Harmonica Summit, where he teaches with other top harmonica pros and connects with students from around the world. He is also a Hohner endorsee and clinician.

Do you play other instruments beside harmonica?

I still play guitar, but that's about it.

What was your path leading up to you as a performer/teacher?

I graduated college with a degree in Spanish language and business. I went on to teach middle school and high school Spanish for a while. That time of my life certainly helped me learn how to become a much better teacher. I also think that learning a foreign language fluently and using it in my travels helped me develop my ear. So, as I began learning harmonica, I also taught others along the way. The teaching has always come naturally to me. I also began performing within that first year of learning to play. I sort of jumped in headfirst with gigging because the opportunities were there.

How did you begin teaching harp?

It wasn't until the year 2000 or so that I began taking students on and teaching actual private lessons. In 2006, I began posting YouTube videos of myself teaching and playing. By 2007, I launched www.harmonica123.com to offer a more comprehensive series of blues-focused harmonica lessons.

How do you teach?

My teaching is based primarily around developing good habits, such as proper technique, and lots of ear training. Judging a student's needs comes from both figuring out what their musical goals and desires are as well as identifying what each player's weaknesses are. I don't necessarily have a set way of teaching, because there are so many different types of learners out there. It's important to understand how folks learn best before developing a plan of attack.

Did you have a teacher, or are you a self-taught harmonica player?

I did have a few teachers who showed me the ropes with the basics, and some intermediate techniques, but I am mostly self-taught. Those early teachers were J. P. Allen, and Michael Rubin. Thanks to those guys, I began developing a solid foundation early on in my playing.

What kind of songs/rhythms do you like to teach best?

It's fun to get players going on a simple train rhythm or chug. This really teaches you how to properly integrate diaphragmatic breathing as a technique into your playing. It's also simple and relaxing to get those chugs going. I also enjoy breaking down solos from some of the greats of blues harmonica.

Who do you suggest students listen to, to get better?

Sonny Boy Williamson I and II, Big Walter Horton, Little Walter, Kim Wilson, George Smith, Gary Primich, Charlie Musselwhite, William Clarke, Paul Delay, and the list goes on and on. I would also recommend that you listen to other genres of music, such as jazz, folk, country, funk, etc. There are many modern players out there today that really bring a unique approach to the instrument, such as Carlos del Junco and Adam Gussow.

Can a Skype lesson be as effective as a lesson in person?

I'm convinced that it comes pretty darn close. The fact that we can both see and hear each other is a huge part of why Skype lessons are so effective. Other than the occasional technological glitches with computers and the internet, it's a great platform to use for teaching/learning.

What are the differences between a Skype lesson and a lesson in person?

Very little. I treat the Skype lessons just like I would a face-to-face lesson. The only difference is that there's no substitute for the quality of audio when working face to face. So, the better the mic you have for your Skype lesson, the better an experience the lesson will be. Same goes for the camera and lighting when it comes to picture quality, but that's less important in my book.

Can you give some specific examples of your teaching method?

When I first begin working with students, I stress the importance of breath control, and I encourage them to work on developing diaphragmatic breathing, slowing down your breath, and controlling it by practicing slow inhale and release of air. The foundation of one's playing is crucial to the future development and evolution of a player's progress as a musician. So, I also work with students to develop proper technique for single notes, bends, holding the harmonica, and working on simple scales/melodies at first. At www.harmonica123.com, I have several different lessons for all levels of players. My focus, however, is blues harmonica lessons geared toward intermediate players. The most popular lessons I sell are the "blues licks" series, where I break down blues riffs note for note and demonstrate them to music so learners have context.

What's the best bit of advice you could give to someone learning to play the harmonica?

Continue to monitor your progress by recording practicing sessions, gigs, and identifying gaps or holes in your playing. Have fun! If it's not fun, you'll never get to where you want to be.

Do you find that many students think they're terrible and talk about giving up harmonica? What do you tell them?

Sure. We've all struggled with learning a new skill or developing our own talent. The key is that your motivation is coming from within. You play and work on your music because it's fulfilling and brings you joy. I also suggest to students that in order to stay motivated, you must seek inspiration often! That's what keeps you going.

How do you have students learn a new song? Tab it? Play it by ear?

I encourage players to both tab and learn by ear. As you learn something by ear, there is no reason why you shouldn't tab it out. I'm not suggesting learning the piece of music from tabs (although sometimes that's best), but rather write them out as you're working on the piece by ear. Then you can go back and play what you've tabbed to see if it matches what you're hearing.

How do you get a student from beginner to intermediate level?

To get from beginner to intermediate, it's important to identify all of your weaknesses and focus the majority of your practice time on those weaknesses, rather than just the things that come easy to you. Furthermore, it must be enjoyable, and integrated in context as you are working on those intermediate techniques. For example, try to always make practice sessions as musical as possible. Try working bends that need improvement into the context of riffs or melodies to practice them.

How do you make intermediate players better?

Helping intermediate players get better is similar to helping a beginner move on to becoming an intermediate player. You still have to identify weaknesses and see how those things fit into your overall musical goals. If you bring it back home, you'll likely stay focused and motivated to improve. My advice to intermediate players is to think about what they would love to be doing with their music and instrument that they're currently not able to do. Then integrate those desires into musical goals, and an action plan. Tackle your goals individually and take your time. Most folks are too anxious and forget to slow down and learn a technique properly before moving on to the next challenge.

And advanced players?

The first thing that comes to mind is phrasing. Musical phrasing develops as a player matures and fully understands the music that he/she is playing. I encourage blues harp players to listen closely to those who have come before them to get new ideas on this topic. Another thing is tone, and pitch control. To be considered an advanced player, you must be able to consistently control the pitch of bends that you play on a diatonic harmonica. Often, tone and pitch go hand in hand and can develop naturally, even when working on them independently.

Who are your favorite harmonica players?

William Clarke, Little Walter, Sonny Boy Williamson II, Kim Wilson, Charlie Musselwhite, James Cotton, Mitch Kashmar, and so many others. It's difficult to list them all.

For advanced, beginners, and intermediates, do you think the kind of harp they play makes a difference?

Yes, I do. Just make sure you're not starting to learn on a five-dollar harmonica. The cheaper the harmonica, the more difficult it is to play and certainly learn on. That doesn't mean that you have to have a customized harmonica or very expensive one, either. Just be sure that it's a quality harmonica between thirty-five and fifty-five dollars, and you'll be fine. The really cheap ones are so leaky that it's hard to even play just a nice, clean note sometimes, and bending can be near impossible.

What brand of harps do you play?

Hohners. I love Crossovers, Special 20s, and Rocket Amp harmonicas the best.

Do you change any of the tunings?

No; in fact, I don't work on my harps at all.

What's the most important thing for harp players to learn, no matter what their ability?

Breath control is number one on my list as a skill. Master your breathing, and you'll be on your way to mastering the instrument. Also, learn how to listen carefully. It's not all about what you play, but more about what you don't play. Lastly, good tone and timing go a long way, so never neglect those concepts.

Do you prefer performing or teaching?

I enjoy them both equally. When I perform, it's the creativity, passion, and connecting with the audience that I enjoy. In teaching, I also find that I can be creative, passionate, and connect with people. I really enjoy the challenge of taking complex concepts or techniques and making them digestible and easy to understand. Come to think of it, when you perform, you're often trying to take the impossible that cannot be expressed in words and communicate those emotions or ideas with your music. Performing and teaching are totally different in some ways, yet they're very similar on certain levels.

You have a CD, *'Til Then*. Is this your first CD?

I've recorded on a handful of other CDs, but this is my first self-released CD with mostly original songs. It can be found at www.ronnieshellist.com. I have some incredible players on that recording: Gerry Hundt on guitar and mandolin, Bob Carter on drums, Todd Edmunds on bass, and Jeremy Vasquez on guitar.

These guys are all incredibly talented and have tons of experience as pro players.

Besides private lessons and the summits and performing, what else are you doing?

Currently, I am busy traveling around the US with Hohner doing training sessions on the Hohner line of harmonicas for various distributors and sales teams, and also putting on presentations at Hohner events. I also host and participate in a handful of in-person workshops and retreats throughout the year in the US, Canada, and Scotland. Everything is all music all the time, and I wouldn't have it any other way.

What has teaching harp done for you?

Without question, it has made me a much better player. It forces me to constantly rethink what I already know. It's a challenge that I really enjoy. It's also given me so much joy to be able to share the knowledge that I have with others. I just love watching folks have that "Aha!" moment. It never gets old. It's also taken me all over the world to meet new people and see new places. Most importantly, my music has allowed me to meet, interact with, and get to know some of my musical heroes. Many have become my closest friends over the years. My heart is full.

Richard Sleigh: Intrepid Harp Tech

Photo courtesy of Karen Pulfer Focht

Richard Sleigh, best known in the harmonica community for his high-performance customized harmonicas, is also a performer who has played on stage with Paquito D'Rivera and the Wooster Symphony Orchestra, Bo Diddley, Taj Mahal, and Maria Muldaur. In addition, he is a guitarist, vocalist, writer, artist, graphic designer, and instructor. He has recorded two solo albums, *Steppin Out* and *Joliet Sessions*, and a collaborative album,

Dennis Gruenling and Richard Sleigh (Backbender Records). And he has recorded for radio and TV and other film projects, playing guitar, slide guitar, harmonica, and penny whistle.

Says Joe Filisko, "Many are aware of Richard Sleigh's reputation as a creative and skillful craftsman, but everyone should also know what a deeply soulful musician he is. All his solo shows have left an indelible mark upon my being." Sleigh's customized harps are played by many famous pro players, such as Howard Levy, Rick Estrin, and Mickey Raphael (Willie Nelson's band). "Richard is one of the world's very best harp techs. He's got a very inventive brain and is always coming up with new tools and ideas," says Brendan Power. Both Power and Sleigh are fascinated with the x-reed type of harmonica, which they feel has a great future, and they've been collaborating together with Hungarian engineer/designer Zombor Kovacs to perfect a small ten-hole x-reed harmonica.

Richard Sleigh grew up in Philipsburg, Pennsylvania, and graduated in 1975 from Pennsylvania State University with a bachelor of fine arts in printmaking and drawing. Almost twenty years later, he moved back to Philipsburg (living next door to his parents) to raise a family and start a new life as a harmonica technician, performing musician, and instructor. He ran his harmonica business from a doctor's office that he converted into a machine shop/music studio.

How did moving back to your family roots affect you?

History came alive for me listening to my mother talk about her father hopping freights during the Depression when he was out of work or handling enough dynamite to blow himself to kingdom come as part of his early-morning job as a coal miner.

Does that explain why you blend trains, music, family history, harmonicas, and railroad history together in your performances and seminars?

Yes. In May 2005, I created a concert, "Songs and Tales of

Trains and Rails," at the Rowland Theater in Philipsburg, Pennsylvania. I handled all aspects of and have also done solo presentations and workshops on railroad history and related music featuring the harmonica, including for students.

As a kid in Philipsburg, what kind of music did you listen to?

I listened to the local radio station—Hank Williams, Patsy Cline, Bill Monroe, Johnny Cash, the Delmore Brothers, Flatt and Scruggs, and a rockin' polka show once a week. Plus, the Reverend Emmeret, who alternated promises of salvation with frequent requests for donations.

What was your first musical instrument, and how old were you?

When I was eight, I got a Roy Rogers Range guitar for Christmas, and my uncle showed me how to play some cowboy chords. I also used the nylon strings of the guitar as a bow to shoot suction-cup arrows at the refrigerator.

How did you happen to get a harmonica, and how old were you when you started playing?

I started playing some rack harmonica—Dylan songs—when I was thirteen. There was a music store in Philipsburg where I took guitar lessons and bought a Marine Band harmonica there, key of C.

Did your family encourage you?

My uncle worked for the Pennsylvania Railroad and played the harmonica—the big Marine Bands, the 364s with the red comb in key of C and G mostly. His two biggest numbers were a steam-train imitation and "The Irish Washerwoman." I learned a bit of a steam-train imitation from him. I also took piano lessons from a concert pianist when I was fourteen. I studied the Mikrokosmos by Béla Bartók and loved it, but my teacher moved away and the other piano teachers in town were boring, so I lost interest and quit. I mostly studied music on my own.

How old were you when you became seriously interested in the diatonic harmonica? What did you do to pursue it?

When I was seventeen at Penn State Altoona Campus, I met Denny Scanlon, who was into Woody Guthrie and Sonny Terry. He spent a summer hopping freight trains, reading *Bound for Glory*, playing guitar and harmonica, and singing. I got infected with his raw enthusiasm and started buying every album that had harmonica on it. *Lost John* with Sonny Terry and Woody Guthrie and the Columbia double album *The Story of the Blues* did it for me. I wore those recordings out listening to them and trying to play along. Then I discovered Little Walter and Charlie McCoy and started playing fiddle tunes. I'd knock myself out trying to find a way to play anything I heard that I liked.

In 1973, you went to the Slade School of Fine Art in London as an exchange student. At the time, you were studying printmaking and drawing in the art department of Penn State University. Were you still playing harp?

I ended up busking on the streets of London. In the spring of 1974, I took off on a racing bike and (with a little help from buses and trains) traveled through Europe with a full set of Marine Band harmonicas, a 270 chromatic, and a couple of penny whistles. I met and jammed with musicians everywhere I went, but Ireland was the high point of my travels musically speaking.

Why was Ireland the high point?

Ireland is permeated with spirits. I get goose bumps just thinking about it. Some are playful, some are very heavy and sad, some are like guardian angels full of wisdom and a reassuring presence. There is an element of music where you become a vehicle for lingering spirits to express themselves through you. I believe this is true no matter where you are, but I discovered this for myself in Ireland in a big way, both by traveling alone and by playing music with other people.

When you were thirteen, you started drinking heavily off and on, and added other drugs to the mix at age seventeen. You finally hit the wall when you were twenty-nine and have been clean ever since. What was that like?

The first four years of staying clean were almost pure white-knuckle insanity. I went to twelve-step meetings constantly but continued to play music. I was doing a solo act and playing in the bars, so now I watched the drinking and getting wasted cycle from a different point of view and was really fascinated and turned off by how ugly things could get at closing time.

How did you overcome the urges?

Reading, which can be like lifting weights. I started reading everything I could find about recovery and spiritual healing, started swimming laps at local pools, called crisis hotlines in the middle of the night, worked the steps. I managed to get through it, and quit smoking tobacco in the bargain. The only mood-altering vice that has stayed with me is coffee

You read two or three books at a time. What else?

I write daily, another way to keep my mind in high creative gear. I want to expose myself to new music and other cultures. I'll try to learn a piece of music that seems impossible to me. Some tunes take years. T-Bone Burnett says there is a kind of blues only a grown man can sing. There are songs that I can inhabit now that sounded shrill and phony when I tried to do them years ago.

You are known as a master harp tech. Did that come about from your interest in the harmonica, or have you always been a tech genius?

The word "genius" makes me laugh. I've always torn things apart to learn how they work, and I am very curious about core principles, but I get saturated quickly if it involves numbers or abstract thought. My main methods are to use my imagination to visualize and do hands-on experimenting. When I work on harmonicas, anything that annoys me about the process becomes the next project. That's how I get obsessed with designing tools and processes.

You went to a SPAH convention and came back with an idea.

I figured out how to build a single cell of a harmonica that let me bend the notes and blow and draw the same way. It had four reeds and two paper valves that I folded into one-way valves in the mouthpiece area. I was convinced that I was going to reinvent the harmonica and become rich and famous.

We know you're famous. Did you become rich?

The rich part has been trickier, but I'm grateful I have found ways to stay in the game. I ended up spending years and thousands of dollars trying things out that did not work. I showed one of my prototypes to Pierre Beauregard and Magic Dick and visited Ned Steinberger and Les Paul, trying to find ways to get it made. That's how I met Joe Filisko—I'd played one of my prototypes in a harmonica blow-off and won a couple of prizes, and Wade Schuman (Hazmat Modine) tipped me to a newspaper piece that mentioned Joe Filisko. I tracked him down and called him up and talked him into looking at my invention.

What happened?

I took a train to Chicago and then to Joliet, Illinois, and spent a weekend with Joe talking harmonica. One thing led to another, and I ended up working with him as a side effect of trying to make this invention get off the ground. Then I learned about Rick Epping's patent and wanted to jump off of a bridge. Later on, I learned about Will Scarlett and Brendan Power figuring out the same thing before I did.

So where is the idea now?

The latest version of this idea is a harmonica developed by Brendan Power and his friend Zombor Kovacs. It's called the MB30—the three of us worked together to build a batch of fifty of these harps and sold them as a limited edition.

Have you switched to this harp exclusively?

I gig with it regularly now. It is incredibly exciting to be relearning how to play the diatonic harmonica with these extra bends and the same tone—well, damn close to the same tone—as my beloved Marine Bands. I still play a lot of "normal" diatonics and some other harps, including the Super 64X chromatic.

How long is the learning curve to be proficient on the MB30?

You can play this harmonica immediately like a normal diatonic, and then start adding the extra bent notes to replace overblows, like playing the major scale in cross harp by bending in the major seventh. Mastering the new possibilities . . . that's another thing altogether. Who knows? I don't. But it is fun to mess with harp players at gigs when they don't know you are playing with an MB30.

What is the difference in tone on your MB30 and on a regular Marine Band?

The MB30 blow notes in the first octave have more punch and a slightly different tone because of the valves. You also end up hitting the notes a little differently because of the valves—the chambers inside the harmonica are also a little different than a standard diatonic, so that might affect tone as well. There is a learning curve to shaping the tone. The same basic elements of technique that create great tone work for the MB30, but you still have to adapt to the instrument.

Do you also have to buy it in every key, or is it like a chromatic harp?

It has the same tuning layout as a standard Richter-tuned diatonic harmonica, so if you really want to convert to the MB30 or some variant of it, you would want to have at least a set of the keys you use most often, if not a full set of all keys.

What are your plans for the MB30?

I want to do whatever I can to make this harp available to more people. It's a tough project, but worth it. I've been at it off and on now for more than thirty years.

And what are Brendan and Zombor doing?

Brendan and Zombor are expanding their experimentations with 3D printers and other technology, as well as various machine shops in the UK and Budapest, Hungary. I'm working with them to develop ideas, work on reed plates, beat the crap out of prototypes at gigs, and report on what's working or not working. We really went through the wringer building the first batch of MB30s, so the goal now is to figure out easier, more cost-effective ways to build the instrument. Plus, make it even more awesome to play.

What are your goals for the future?

To create a body of instructional materials and tools that make harp tech something anyone who plays the instrument can do, starting with basic tuning and adjusting and going from there as far as you want to go. I've been working for years on a series of exercises for building the rest of the instrument—your body—to amplify and bring out your personal version of rich, full, relaxed, gorgeous tone. This includes posture, breathing, and the muscles of the vocal tract. Combine these with other warmup exercises like pentatonic scales, chord rhythms, and metronome work to give people a foundation on the harmonica that they can go in any direction with. Get these concepts really dialed in, in a way that others can use them easily, no matter what level they are at. I want to play music with great musicians, make some new recordings, and nail down some things on x-reed harps that give people an idea of where they can go with this new harp. Ry Cooder did an album called *Chicken Skin Music*—music that gives you goose bumps. I want to play THAT kind of music as often as possible, roots music that connects people with each other and with their own aliveness.

Why is breath so important?

We are lucky to play an instrument that makes you focus on the breath and makes you breathe music. Your breath is your power. Get into it! General Patton used to say that oxygen feeds the brain. It is so true and so easy to forget. Breathe deeper, think deeper, live deeper. You can use the harmonica as a way to remember how powerful your breath can be.

How can people get in touch with you?

My email is rrsleigh@gmail.com. My main website is hotrodharmonicas.com.

Chapter 29

Kim Wilson: Soul of the Fabulous Thunderbirds

Photo courtesy of Joseph A. Rosen

Founding member (along with guitarist Jimmie Vaughan) of the Austin, Texas, blues-rock band the Fabulous Thunderbirds, Detroit-born Kim Wilson is also a virtuoso solo blues harmonica player, singer, and songwriter. For nearly two decades he has fronted the various Fabulous Thunderbirds band members and has guested (as a vocalist or harp player) on albums of Carlos Santana, Paul Simon, and Albert Collins.

In 1990 when the Thunderbirds took a hiatus, Wilson joined Dave Edmunds' Rock 'n' Roll Revue with Graham Parker, Steve Cropper, and Dion DiMucci. Three years later, Wilson began his solo recording career with *Tigerman*, followed by *That's Life* in 1994. His 2001 album, *Smokin' Joint*, was nominated for a Grammy Award and several W. C. Handy Awards. In 2001, he performed on Woody Guthrie's tribute album, *Daddy-O Daddy! Rare Family Songs of Woody Guthrie*.

In 2003, M.C. Records released *Lookin' for Trouble*, featuring nine songs written or cowritten by Wilson and five cover songs by such blues masters as Snooky Pryor, L. C. McKinley, and Willie Dixon. While Wilson's playing has been compared to Little Walter, Wilson says he has been more influenced by Muddy Waters, and told NPR, "I think that you have so many influences and you steal so much stuff that finally it just gets mixed up into you." He also insisted that it would be impossible to imitate other great harmonica players because, Wilson says, "the notes you're playing only happen once."

Your father was an executive with General Motors, but also sang songs on the radio?

My dad had a regular day job. He didn't graduate from high school, but started working for GM when he was sixteen years old and was singing on the radio. He actually sang with Danny Thomas on the radio.

So how did your musical career begin?

In Detroit, we had mandatory music once or twice a week where a bunch of kids would toot around on their ocarinas all at one time. One day the teacher picked me out, handed me a baritone horn, and said, "Play it." So I played it and was immediately first chair. That's when I got started playing music.

I was studying trombone and guitar when I was eight. I took lessons all the way until the end of junior high, when we moved to California. I wanted to be an athlete; I was a pretty good football player and had scholarships to play ball in college, but right after high school I picked up the harmonica, and in a month, I was in a band. In a year, I was playing with all the old guys like Eddie Taylor, Peewee Creighton, Albert Collins, Ralph Wilson—and then it just went on from there.

How did you happen to pick up the harmonica?

Blues was a big thing back in the mid to late sixties. All the old guys were playing around. I picked it up and got halfway decent pretty quickly. Everybody else thought I was great, but I wasn't. Then I went to Santa Barbara City College for about half of a semester and didn't show up a lot. And then I went, "You know what? I'm playing music."

You called yourself Goleta Slim and played with George "Harmonica" Smith.

In 1970, my buddy started calling me Goleta Slim, and it stuck. I played in Goleta (in the Santa Barbara area) until 1972, and then I moved to Minnesota. I went up there, made a little money, not much—there wasn't much to be made back then—and I stayed for about a year and a half. These guys came to Minnesota. Willie Dixon had heard a tape I'd done at a studio where we cut some songs, and he offered to be my manager. He wasn't my manager very long; he didn't have time for me. He put me onto Jimmy Reed's manager, who got me involved with these guys who had the fifth-largest black-owned business in the United States—fire prevention. They wanted to start a blues label, so they handed me fifty bucks, bought me a new suit, and I was theirs. I made this 45rpm with them, and they flew me out to Seattle, where they were based. We did a big show with Howlin' Wolf, John Lee Hooker, Albert Collins, Margie Evans—all these great people.

Jimmie Vaughan had come to visit and sat in with my band for three nights. We got really drunk and started talking about Texas. After the Seattle show, I told the guys I was going to visit my girlfriend in San Francisco, and I went to Texas instead. We decided to start the Thunderbirds. I went back to Minnesota and told those guys I was leaving. I drove to Texas with an amp and records and a few clothes, that was it.

After you moved to Texas, you were tutored by Muddy Waters, Jimmy Rogers, Eddie Taylor, Albert Collins—what was the most important thing you learned from them?

Those guys were great people; they were very humble—they'd been ripped off. They taught me how to be a human, and that was more than any musical thing I could learn.

You said, "I turned off my radio in 1972 and withdrew into my closet to play every kind of low-down thing." Was that low-down blues?

That's blues. I call it low-down. I tried to learn every style I could. I realized that I wasn't going to have a life stealing solos off records, and I really did work on my own thing. Basically, it was just keeping a harmonica in my mouth the whole time. Unfortunately, I was heavily self-medicated a lot of those years between '71 and '88. Luckily, I had a harmonica in my mouth the whole time, because in '74, when I moved to Texas, that's when I met all these old guys, which was the greatest thing that ever happened to me.

You played with Muddy in the seventies, and he called you the world's best. What was it like to play with Muddy?

Muddy was very special because harmonica was the solo instrument in his band, and he took a liking to me. Back then it wasn't true, but he said I was the best since Little Walter. It wasn't true, but ever since then, I've strived to be as good as what he thought I was back then. And hopefully, it's kind of working out for me now.

Did Muddy ask you to play like any of his previous harp players? Or were you free to create your own sound?

He didn't ask, but there's certain things that belong on certain songs, and I would just embellish them. I was just a kid, twenty-four years old. I was already on my way to doing my own thing. Obviously, my influences are apparent in my playing: Little Walter, of course, James Cotton, George Harmonica Smith, Louisiana, people like Lazy Lester and Slim Harpo, Junior Parker, Sonny Boy Williamson (Rice Miller, who really was my guide as far as the Sonny Boys go), Snooky Pryor, Big Walter Horton. There are a lot of different people I tap into when I play. When I hit octaves, it's very George Statuesque. When I play the chromatic, it's pretty much the combination of George Smith and Little Walter together, because those were the guys on the chromatic harmonica for blues.

Do you prefer chromatic or diatonic?

I play both. I play more diatonic; it just goes with the music more. I love to play the chromatic harmonica. I play it in the blues style. I play it in D and E flat, I don't do much—I'll use the button. I'll get a major third sometimes, but I'll hit some transitional things with the button also. It's a lot like the organ: a lot of chords, not as many single notes, a lot of octaves, because that's the George Smith style, and that's something I really like. People don't even realize that I can play the chromatic harmonica.

You opened for Eric Clapton in 1982. Did you have any rapport with him?

I had some; he hired me to play on one of his records recently. When we first got hooked up, we played two separate tours, one in '81 and one in '83. He had to cancel the last few gigs of the one in '81 because he was sick with ulcers. I think he was also self-medicating, but he had to cancel a lot of his shows. He rehired us in '83 and was totally straight. I think Clapton is one of these guys who's gone in a lot of different directions musically, and he's legitimized every single one of them.

Besides harmonica and harmonica players, what instruments and instrumentalists influenced your approach to blues harp playing?

I like sax players and certain guitarists. I'll go into a T-Bone Walker thing sometimes. I love Illinois Jacquet, and Gene Adams. I listen to him all the time. I listen to a lot of music constantly, all the people who are my heroes, and also, I listen just for the enjoyment. I love blues music, but I love all music: I love good soul music, I love jazz—the older jazz. I love Lee Morgan on the trumpet. Kenny Burrell and Grant Green on guitar. Jimmy Smith and Brother Jack McDuff—those are my two favorite organ players. To me, Jimmy Smith is still the guy; he was the greatest, most innovative, most exciting guy on the organ.

Let's talk about the Fabulous Thunderbirds a little. In 1974, you went to Texas and became the house band at Antone's. What was that like?

It was fantastic. We played with Albert Collins, Eddie Taylor, and Jimmy Rogers. I was always hanging around that club drinking wine. I had nothing else to do, so I'd hang around and meet all these guys. That's where I met Muddy. It was a playground—guys like Earl King would come in, and I'd ask him about Smiley Lewis and he'd tell me Smiley Lewis stories; I'd get him all fired up and he'd get up there and go crazy. People like Clarence Hollimon, who ended up playing on one of my Antone's records, and Carol Fran, his wife. I did some stuff with Buddy Guy. I was hanging around with Willie "Big Eyes" Smith and Calvin "Fuzz" Jones, Jerry Portnoy—it was a dream that Clifford

Antone created for all of us. It was his baby. He loved the music—God bless him—I miss him. I miss him bad. But I miss all the people who have gone, because they were the ones who really made it happen for me. It's a difficult world to live in now because all the old guys are gone. I'm the old guy. I lived to play with those guys; I lived to please them. I didn't really care about a fucking audience; all I cared about was Muddy Waters, Jimmy Rogers, Eddie Taylor, Buddy Guy, and all the great guys we played with.

Jimmie Vaughan left the Thunderbirds in 1989. Why did he leave, and have you played together since then?

He left because it was time for him to leave. Has he been replaced? Over and over again, with great musicians. For me, during that period of time, it was really time to clean house, and that's what I ended up doing. I felt like I needed to move on with my musical life. Now I've got a couple guys from Texas, who are fantastic. I'm old enough now to say, "This is about me. This is about making me happy." There've been a lot of great musicians, and you need to have reverence for the past, but you need to move on and let go.

With the Fabulous Thunderbirds, there's no set list, you just wing it every night; you call out a key and you start playing, and the band has to follow. What's the advantage of doing that?

Well, the advantage is that it's satisfying to me and to the audience—they don't get the same show every night. I mean, I'll call off songs. I won't always just start playing. I'll figure out what the audience wants, and I'll call the songs according to what I'm feeling they want.

Do you play with your eyes open all the time? Can you concentrate as much with your eyes open?

That's an interesting question. I'm usually watching the guitar player's hands when I'm backing people up. When I take a solo, I go into the zone. If you know the song well enough, you go into the zone anyway.

What do you think is the future of blues?

I'm not going to say it has no future, but there are not many people playing blues these days. They're saying they're playing it, but they're not. I think you could see it go away, but it's not going to go away until after I croak. The problem is there are no singers out there really singing blues; you've got people singing R&B, soul, gospel-y kinds of things. Some of it's kind of pseudo. But nobody's really singing blues, and that's where I come in because I'm a blues singer. I'll mess with the soul stuff. But every time I go into a contemporary record, it's a blues singer singing soul music; I'll get a little soul-y with it, but consequently, it comes out pretty unique. You can't be unique until you're well-versed in tradition.

Your style of blues playing has been described as loaded with the textures of a full-blown horn section. How do you get your incredible tone?

It's a physical thing. I like richness, I like to be able to get a lot of different kinds of sounds on the harmonica. A lot of these guys go out, and it's always distorted. I don't like that all the time. I like giving a lot of sounds—that's one thing Little Walter was fantastic at. Of course, Little Walter just played on whatever they threw at him. There were times, I think, when Little Walter was playing through a cardboard box with a speaker in it, but he made it sound good. The Chess Brothers were geniuses. They were just as valuable as any musician—they really made that stuff larger than life.

What kind of harps do you play?

They're Marine Bands, but Joe Filisko works on all my

harmonicas. He's a genius working on harmonicas, and he's a genius player too, a great player. I got in on the ground floor with Joe. He's a fantastic technician, an engineer. I tried doing that stuff myself, but it's impossible. I tried taking one of his apart one time—that was a nightmare. I just play them.

What does music mean to you?

Music is life. Music is religion. You get very close to God when you're really playing. You're seeing God. You're hanging with him. When you're in the zone on that bandstand, that's as close to heaven as you can get and be alive on this planet.

Chapter 30

Winslow Yerxa: The Musician's Musician

"I can think of few musicians by my definition as complete as Winslow Yerxa," says Jason Ricci. "Part mad scientist, part historian, part educator, but always an artist. I believe Winslow's borderline obsessive and totally thorough knowledge of the harmonica is unmatched by anyone alive, and he's one of the most surprising, unique and artistic players I've ever heard. The culture, history, and traditions he digests so completely radiate through his educational escapades, innovations, and music." Adds Ricci, "Winslow is also much more mischievous than many people realize, though most his jokes go over our head."

Winslow Yerxa is a musician's musician, a master of French and French Canadian styles, fiddle tunes, Scottish, jazz, and blues. He is the author of three books: *Harmonica for Dummies*, *Harmonica for Dummies, Second Edition*, and *Blues Harmonica for Dummies*. He is the cofounder, along with Jason Ricci, of the Harmonica Collective, a three-day intensive yearly harmonica workshop. Yerxa offers video and audio products at www.winslowyerxa.com and is a resident expert at www.bluesharmonica.com. In addition, he is a former contributor to Mel Bay Harmonica Sessions webzine and publisher of HIP, the Harmonica Information Publication. He teaches both in person and online in San Francisco and at the Jazzschool Community Music School in Berkeley, California. Yerxa served as president of SPAH from 2012 to 2015.

You were exposed to music when you were how old?

Probably since birth. It's a very musical family.

What was your first instrument, and how old were you?

I had basic piano lessons when I was about eleven for a few months, but nobody forced me to continue, so I gave that up. Then, when I was about fourteen, I was listening to a lot of pop radio and started singing. I got into a garage band, where I was the lead singer. There were harmonica parts in a lot of the music that we were playing, largely drawn from British blues rock bands emulating American blues. At first, I hummed this electric kazoo for the harmonica parts, but after a while, I thought I should actually get a harmonica, asked someone what I should get, and was told, "Go get a C harp." I didn't tell him I was trying to play a song in E, and that sort of worked and sort of didn't. That began the cognitive dissonance that turned into this lifelong quest. Eventually, I found if you want to play the blues in E, you get an A harp. So, in a real sense, harmonica was my first actual instrument.

Did you have a teacher, or are you self-taught?

Self-taught. There simply weren't any teachers around.

How did you learn?

Well, some from just picking up little pieces of advice. When I first found out about second position, or the cross harp, as it was primarily known then, I went into a music store and the guy said, "Oh, there's this thing called cross harp, and by the way, there's this book by this guy named Tony Glover called *Blues Harp*." That was very helpful. I got an A harp, and now I could play in E and the chords didn't sound weird. Tony Glover's book gave me a lot on the history and general lore, but I don't recall learning very much from it technically. I basically had to teach myself. I have the kind of mind that can very easily pick up on things like music theory, so I was able to kind of make sense of how things worked musically and how the harmonica fit into that. I had to figure out a lot of things. Sometimes I would have questions that people really couldn't answer, like the idea of corner-switching, playing alternately out of the left or the right corner of the mouth with the tongue in the middle. I remember stumbling on that and thinking, *God, is this a blind alley, or is this worth developing?* It turns out it was worth developing, but I had no way of knowing.

I've actually had one formal harmonica lesson in my entire life. We talked a lot of harmonica lore. I played a little bit for him. About the only advice he gave me was learn to play a little faster. I had all sorts of questions, but he said, "No, you'll do fine." That was the lesson.

Who do you listen to for inspiration?

That can come from anywhere. It might come from Robert Johnson on one day and from Sofi Tukker another day. It's a duo, a woman named Sophie Hawley-Weld, who sings and plays guitar, and a man named Tucker Halpern, who does everything else. One of the things I've noticed in a lot of these duos is that basically, there's not a lot of playing of instruments. There's a lot of sampling and electronica, which leaves the duo, who don't have a back-up band, to do a whole lot of jumping around on stage. There's another one from South Africa called the Die Antwoord. Again, a man and a woman, bizarre-looking people who jump around a lot, but they make some pretty interesting music. Several months ago, Jason played a show in San Francisco. I went, "What the heck is that? Because I liked it." So, I typed their lyrics into a Google search, and up came this group.

Do you practice daily?

I don't even play harmonica every day. Sometimes I'll think about it. I'll actually do scale-based exercises in my head. The other morning, I woke up thinking about playing scale-based patterns in the key of B on the chromatic harmonica. Just because B major is a weird key most players shy away from. And I thought, *Okay, here's this little exercise. Let me just do it in my head.* Later, I did play it on the chromatic. But I'm not somebody who practices obsessively. I go through periods of it.

Who do you suggest that students listen to in order to improve their playing?

If you want to play blues, listen to the greats. If you want to play other kinds of music, find out if there is harmonica in it, and listen to those people. But two things: be critical. Just because somebody's playing harmonica doesn't mean that either it's the best possible use of it in the music or that there isn't something that could be done drawing from the music in general, rather than just from the people who play harmonica. And if there isn't harmonica in the music, figure out how harmonica could fit into it. There's a leap of imagination that can be made in any musical circumstance.

Can you give a specific example of your teaching method?

Well, it's pretty general. I try and find out, what inspires someone to play? It could be a kind of music, a specific player; it could be a very specific goal, like, I want to play Christmas carols for the family gathering. It could be they just like the sound of the harmonica, or they always wanted to play an instrument. It's good to know that. And two, do they have a harmonica? If so, what kind, and what has been their experience, if any, trying to play it so far?

Another thing I found very important, especially with adult beginners, is what other musical activities they've engaged in. Because one of the things that I found is that people come to wanting to play music from having no musical background. And therefore, no idea of basic concepts. I learned a bit about that when I wrote the first edition of *Harmonica for Dummies*. I learned, don't assume anything about a student.

What's the best piece of advice you could give to someone learning to play the harmonica?

Harmonica is the tip of the iceberg.

What do you mean?

Well, 90 percent of the iceberg is below the surface of the water and invisible. Ninety percent of the harmonica happens inside your body. Pay attention to what's happening as the air moves from the bottom of your lungs, up through your throat, past your tongue, and out through your lips, or going in the opposite direction and through the harmonica. Because that entire chain produces the sound.

What are your tips for becoming a better player?

Listen to yourself and listen to others. One of the things I feel really fortunate about is that when I was a teenager listening to harmonica players, I had the very good fortune of hearing not only good blues harmonica players, but also really good chromatic players. Sometimes I didn't know who I was listening to. But I heard such great examples that I emulated it, and that helped my playing a lot.

Listening to yourself is an important part of developing your playing, and recording yourself is a hugely useful tool. I sometimes wonder how anybody got to be any good at playing an instrument before they could record themselves and listen back, because you'll hear two things when you listen back: you'll hear the cringe-worthy moments when you realize, "Oh my God. I sound like that?" But you'll also hear the moments when you realize, "Wow! That sounds way better than I thought."

When you're playing, there's your experience of how you feel about what you're doing at the moment, and then there's your listening experience. The two don't always match. You may think you sound terrible, but you actually sound pretty good. But your experience of what you're going through to produce that, the uncertainty, the doubt, the difficulties you're facing technically, may mask the fact that you're actually sounding good. By recording yourself and listening back, you'll hear places where you're really good and you hear the places where you really need to work on stuff and improve.

How do you cultivate relaxation?

Breathing.

What about those "type As" that don't relax?

Good question. I think physical awareness of your body is really the key to that. There's mental relaxation and there's physical relaxation, but I think the physical can help induce the mental. And if you're aware of your breathing . . . I went through this recently over the holidays. I was feeling heartsick about things that were going on in my life. I was lying in bed, and I realized, that's located right at the bottom of the apex of my rib cage. And if I breathe fully, I can let go of that feeling. That emotion was actually centered in a part of my body. And that really helped me a lot.

But then, you can radiate out from the breathing. How do your shoulders feel? How do your leg muscles and arm muscles feel? How does your neck feel? How does your throat feel? There's all these points in the body that can become tense. And if you can release those through awareness part by part, then you can induce relaxation.

Have you ever had a period when you were uninspired, feeling as though you were playing the same old riffs?

That can happen at any point. You can get stuck in a little rut. And there are many ways out of that. In a practice situation, you can just say, "Okay, let me do something totally unfamiliar." Sometimes play something on another instrument. I'll sit down at the piano, typically. To me, that's the most accessible instrument, more so than guitar, though I play a little bit of guitar. I'll come up with patterns that I'd never think of on the harmonica. And then I can transfer them to the harmonica. Or I might just hear a line in my head and sing it. So that's one way of breaking out of a rut.

One of the things that will happen on any instrument, including harmonica, is that you get into a physical routine of playing a sequence of actions. And that sequence of actions is going to bring you to a sequence of notes. And if those actions become habitual, then you're going to be in a bit of a rut. There's a physical way out of that, and that is to say, "Okay. I'm going to play a consistent series of unfamiliar actions, and they're going to be completely arbitrary." Like, "I'm going to blow in this hole, and then the next hole I'm going to draw, and then the hole after that, I'm going to blow again," something like that. It will produce a different series of note patterns as you go up the harmonica. Because at least on the diatonic harmonica, every octave is tuned differently. The note layout changes. It's not like the piano, where it's staying from octave to octave. So you're going to get different results.

Consistent physical actions produce different musical results. So you can actually play arbitrary patterns on the harmonica and generate new licks. That's another way of doing it. There are lots of ways out of that. When playing in a performing situation, that can be different. There's a certain amount of adrenaline that comes from playing live in front of people. This is something I'm trying to work through. It reduces my IQ by about fifty points, because you're in "fight or flight" mode. You grasp on to whatever little thing you can cling to, and that often is a familiar pattern, one of those habitual, boring patterns that you know really well, and have worn smooth over time. That can serve you well in terms of not falling out of the music. But it can also mean that you're doing something that's kind of boring and threadbare.

You play both diatonic and chromatic. Which do you think is harder to play?

Both, equally. I started both almost simultaneously, and I find that they're actually different instruments in the same family. Each offers different advantages and disadvantages, and each has its own set of difficulties.

So, if you were going to get up on stage, you would depend on what song they were playing, and choose to play diatonic or chromatically?

Pretty much. And I might make a different choice on the same song in a different situation. There's also a social aspect to this. If I'm among other harmonica players, I'll choose to do what nobody else is doing. In a harmonica player social situation, I'll play tremolo, I'll play whatever I think can produce something different within the music. It's fun to do. It makes it more interesting.

What has music done for you?

It's given me focus in my life.

Acknowledgments

First, I would like to thank Joe Rosen, photographer extraordinaire, who shot photos of ten of the interviewees. His contributions are every bit as important as the players and teachers interviewed in this book. And I would like to thank my harmonica buddy, Kris Ciesiga, who shot the cover photo for the book. I would also like to thank Matt Peyton for taking the time to shoot my author shot one night while I was jamming.

This book would never have been possible without the help of so many people who have encouraged me on both my harmonica and writing journey. I thank Jon Gindick for encouraging me, as a raw beginner, to learn to draw the two-note. I gratefully thank my harp teacher and friend, Lee Edwards, who continues to guide my musical journey and stops me from criticizing my playing. I thank SPAH, especially J. P. Pagan, who was then the editor of *Harmonica Happenings*, and Winslow Yerxa, former president of SPAH and the human encyclopedia of all things harmonica.

I thank the house band at Big Ed's World Famous Blues Jam at the Red Lion on Bleecker Street who encourage me every Monday night, especially Big Ed. When I first went to his jam, I'd only been playing a year, but signed up. When I heard the band play, I scratched my name off the list and tried to sneak out. Big Ed saw me at the door and said, "Leaving so soon?" I replied, "When I can play half as well as you guys, I'll return." Big Ed said, "Just play like you." Thanks to Big Ed Sullivan, I've tried to ever since. The entire house band has been so encouraging: keyboardist David Bennett Cohen (formerly of Country Joe and the Fish) always whispers helpful hints to me. Matt Mousseu, the in-the-pocket drummer, and his wife, Grammy-nominated Christine Santelli, both give me endless support. Bass player Arthur Neilson (Shemekia Copeland's guitarist) always ups my game every time I get to play with him. And harmonicist jammer David

Barnes and drummer jammer Mike Rodbard are always so encouraging. But especially, I thank Big Ed, who always asks me after I play, "Did you have fun?" And these days, the answer is always "Yes!"

I thank Jimmy Mack of Jimmy Mack and the Boys at the Farside Jam in Hoboken, New Jersey, for his constant encouragement, and Ross Daisomont, front man of Radio Flyer Blues Jam at American Trash, NYC, who has created the best tip jar in the country, and Tim Frost and Mike Berman at Cassidy's NYC jam for their continuing support.

I thank my fellow writers—Judy Kirkwood, Mickey Goodman, Hilary Nangle, Echo Garrett, and Irene Levine—for their excellent advice and ongoing encouragement. I thank author Sherry Suib Cohen and problem-solver Sue Cohen, who always have my back. I thank my editor at *Business Jet Traveler*, Jeff Burger, who is a superb editor, and my good friend Maren Rudolph for her ongoing encouragement. And I thank my superstar endocrinologist, Dr. Jason Baker, who sees to it that I remain in top physical condition.

I thank Drew Lewis at Hohner, who has supplied me with enough harmonicas for entire classrooms in Papua New Guinea, Colombia, Uganda, and the Republic of Georgia to introduce our little instrument throughout the world.

There are many other people who have helped me on my harp journey: Tom Halchek of Blue Moon Harmonicas (I won his custom Manji A flat with the cool pink comb in the Great Comb Debate, Golden Ear Award at SPAH), Ron Hobdy of Rockin' Rons Music (who sends me harps as fast as I blow them out), and Greg Heumann of BlowsMeAway Productions, who made my magnificent custom wood Stealth mic with my initials, MG, like the car logo.

I thank all the players and teachers who have helped me in various harmonica workshops, especially Jason Ricci, Todd Parrott, Ronnie Shellist, Joe Filisko, Dennis Gruenling, Richard Sleigh, Winslow Yerxa, Buzz Krantz, Jon Gindick, and so many more for their excellent guidance and advice. You've all made this journey so fun and worthwhile.

Acknowledgments

    Finally, I would like to thank all the wonderful people at Mountain Arbor Press.

    Creating a book takes an entire team, the same way creating music takes an entire band. I used to think when I got up to jam that it was all about my harp solo: Was it good? Was it horrible? But I've finally learned, it's not about me—it's about what I contribute to make the entire band sound great.

About the Author

Margie Goldsmith, winner of the Society of American Travel Writers Gold Lowell Thomas Award and eighty-four other writing awards, has hiked, biked, climbed, paddled, and luxuriated in 140 countries on seven continents and written about them all for *Travel + Leisure, Robb Report, American Way, Hemispheres, Islands, Wall Street Journal, The Globe and Mail, New York Times*, and many others. She is a contributing lifestyle writer for Forbes.com and writes features and a museum column for *Business Jet Traveler*. She specializes in experiential travel and interviews with CEOs, celebrities, and musicians, including Francis Ford Coppola, Sir Richard Branson, Harry Connick Jr., Robert Herjavec, and many others. Goldsmith is a triathlete and marathoner, has climbed to Advanced Base Camp of the north face of Mt. Everest, practices kickboxing, and plays blues harmonica.

Other Books by Margie Goldsmith

Screw-Up

www.ingramcontent.com/pod-product-compliance
Lightning Source LLC
Chambersburg PA
CBHW070049080526
44586CB00013B/972